LEARNING TO DRIVE A CAR

Údarás Um Shábháilteacht Ar Bhóithre
Road Safety Authority

First published by Údarás Um Shábháilteacht Ar Bhóithre / Road Safety Authority 2012

© 2012 Údarás Um Shábháilteacht Ar Bhóithre / Road Safety Authority

ISBN 978-0-9567931-0-2

10 9 8 7 6 5 4 3 2 1

Údarás Um Shábháilteacht Ar Bhóithre
Road Safety Authority

Páirc Ghnó Ghleann na Muaidhe, Cnoc an tSabhaircín,
Bóthar Bhaile Átha Cliath, Béal an Átha, Co. Mhaigh Eo.

Moy Valley Business Park, Primrose Hill, Dublin Road,
Ballina, Co. Mayo.

locall: 1890 50 60 80   fax: (096) 25 252
email: info@rsa.ie   website: www.rsa.ie

Every effort has been made to ensure the accuracy and reliability of information contained in this book. The Road Safety Authority cannot accept responsibility for any inaccuracies or errors, and any reliance that readers place in this book or in the information contained in it is at their own risk. Information in this book is for guidance only.

In no event will the Road Safety Authority be liable for any loss or damage, including without limitation, indirect or consequential loss or damage, or any loss or damage whatsoever arising out of, or in connection with the use of this book.

Foreword

Building a strong safety culture on Irish roads is the core mission of the RSA, one that is centred very firmly on drivers and their behaviour on the road.

Research from all around the world tells us that the manner in which people learn to drive is a key factor in their future behaviour on the road – they are more likely to be safe and competent behind the wheel when they have learned within a staged and formal process, and where they have taken responsibility for their own learning experience.

The purpose of this book is to help learner drivers to do just that and to work with a registered ADI and a sponsor to step through the various stages in learning how to drive. As part of regular driving instruction or during the Essential Driver Training programme, an ADI will help you learn the basic skills. Your sponsor is typically an experienced driver who is prepared to make the commitment to help you develop your skills and knowledge so that you can become a safe and competent driver.

Learning to drive will give you a great sense of independence, but with that independence comes responsibility – for your own safety and that of other road users. Every time you sit into the driver's seat of a car, you are accepting that responsibility.

Encouraging learner drivers to take responsibility for their own learning is at the heart of this book. Learners are asked to make commitments about what they have learnt and about their own future behaviour. Your ADI and sponsor will help you to acquire the skills and knowledge you need to make each of these commitments.

In today's world, being able to drive is a valuable life skill, one that can enhance your personal and your working life. We are confident that this book can make a contribution to improving Irish road safety. We wish all learner drivers many years of safe driving.

Noel Brett, Chief Executive Officer, RSA

Contents

Using this book 7
    Chapter by chapter 7
    What else you should read 8

1. Getting yourself organised 9
    Learning and doing 9
    Recording your progress: making commitments 9
    Competencies: things to know and things to do 10
    Learning in a structured way 11
    Who's going to help you? 12
    Stages in learning to drive 15
    The learner driver and the law 16

2. Controls and manoeuvring the car 18
    Basic car knowledge 18
    Know your car – before you turn on the engine 21
    Starting and stopping the car: the first time 24
    Your first time on the road 29

3. Gaining experience on the road 31
    Planning practice journeys 31
    Reading the road 32
    Knowing your position on the road 34
    Dealing with junctions 36
    Controlling your speed 42
    Signalling your intentions 44
    Reversing 47
    Parking 49
    Overtaking 52
    Starting on a hill 53
    Turning the car around 54
    Stopping in an emergency 55
    Driving on motorways 56

Údarás Um Shábháilteacht Ar Bhóithre
Road Safety Authority

4. Dealing with more challenging conditions 59
Dealing with hazards 59
Driving in heavy traffic 60
Night-time driving 61
Driving in conditions of poor visibility 64
Driving in poor on-road conditions 67
Dealing with road works and other obstructions 69
Town and country: challenges of urban and rural driving 71

5. Sharing the road 74
Making sure you're fit to drive 74
Staying calm: showing courtesy 77
Avoiding and dealing with distractions while driving 78
Dealing with other road users 80
Thinking of the environment 84
Dealing with collisions and emergencies 87

Summary of commitments 89

Using this book

You've made the big step of deciding that you want to learn how to drive. You've been looking forward to getting behind the wheel for quite some time now, you're eager to get started, and you're probably also a little nervous.

To become a safe and competent driver, you need:

- To learn – about the *Rules of the Road*, about your car, about the law;
- To get the support of a sponsor and of an Approved Driving Instructor (ADI);
- To plan a programme of learning; and
- To practise, practise and practise again.

Road safety organisations around the world have tried to find out what makes people good and safe drivers. One of the things they discovered is that the way people learn how to drive is extremely important. In particular, one thing is clear – learners become better and safer drivers when they have gone through a structured and planned learning programme.

The purpose of this book is to help you to take responsibility for your own learning, to plan your own programme of activity (with your sponsor) and to develop your driving skills safely and efficiently. You won't learn how to drive just by reading about it – but if you plan how you learn to drive, the chances are you'll become a safe, competent and responsible driver.

Chapter by chapter

This book presents a typical path that you might follow as a learner driver.

1. Getting yourself organised: this chapter deals with how you (as the learner) can take responsibility for your own learning. It covers getting the support of a sponsor and planning a programme of learning. It also covers the legal and safety requirements that you need to think about.

2. Controls and manoeuvring the car: this chapter covers how you can learn the basic skills that you need to control and manoeuvre your car – how to start and stop, steer, change gears, position your car on the road, keep up with traffic, and so on. It also covers things you need to know about your car's controls and some basic information about maintenance and safety checks.

3. Gaining experience on the road: this chapter describes how you can put what you know in theory into practice in real 'on the road' practice sessions with your sponsor. It covers the different types of road and road layout that you will come across, and describes how you can learn to share the road safely with other road users, including other drivers, cyclists and pedestrians. This chapter also covers some more difficult driving skills that you need to learn, including starting on a hill, parking and reversing.

4. Dealing with more challenging conditions: this chapter takes what you've learned in chapters 2 and 3 and applies them to more difficult or challenging conditions – including bad weather, driving at night, driving in heavy traffic, and driving on different types of road.

5. Sharing the road: this chapter looks at some of the personal qualities you need to develop to become a consistently safe and competent driver. These include the ability to stay calm under pressure, to treat other road users with courtesy and respect, and to commit yourself to driving only when you are physically and mentally fit to do so safely. It also looks at things you can do to reduce the impact of your driving on the environment. Lastly it gives some tips on what to do if you are the first person at the scene of a collision.

What else you should read

Before you start to learn to drive, there's a lot you can do to prepare.

- You need to have an excellent knowledge of the *Rules of the Road*. Keep a copy handy, as you will need to refer to it often while you are learning how to drive.
- If you are learning to drive in your own car or in that of a family member or friend, make sure to read the car's user manual.
- The RSA publishes leaflets on a wide range of topics relating to road safety and driver licensing. These are available on the RSA's website and in public libraries, post offices, Garda stations and other public places.
- The RSA website is packed with resources for drivers and learner drivers. These include tips and hints on road safety, information about the driving tests and lists of Approved Driving Instructors for every county. You can also download the *Rules of the Road* and other documents from the website. You can also look at road safety videos.

1. Getting yourself organised

In this chapter

This chapter deals with how you (as the learner) can take responsibility for your own learning. You do this in a number of ways:

- By getting the support of a sponsor who will coach you in the skills of driving, help you to develop good driving habits, and help you plan a structured programme of learning;
- By following a course of driving instruction with an Approved Driving Instructor (ADI); and
- By taking the Essential Driver Training (EDT) programme – this is mandatory for learners with first-time learner permits with a start date on or after 4 April 2011. See **www.rsa.ie** for more information.

This chapter also covers the legal and safety requirements that you need to know. You must understand the serious responsibilities you are taking on when you are learning to drive.

Learning and doing

Learning to drive a car is a serious undertaking. There are so many things to learn and remember, and so many things to do and practise. You want to learn and practise within a structured environment that will help you to develop good and safe driving habits. Driving a car safely and competently is about much more than just controlling or manoeuvring the car – you need to develop a wide range of skills, such as:

- Observation skills – noticing what other road users are doing or are about to do;
- Judgement skills – that enable you to know what's the right thing to do in different circumstances;
- Planning skills – that help you to prepare for different manoeuvres and routes;
- Anticipation skills – that help you to avoid hazards; and
- Reaction skills – that enable you to take evasive action in good time in the event of a dangerous situation or an emergency.

You will also begin to understand how correct driver behaviour and a correct attitude will help you become a competent driver.

Recording your progress: making commitments

When you learn to drive, you learn to take responsibility. This includes responsibility for keeping track of your own learning, and being honest with yourself about the progress you are making.

Throughout this book there are '**My commitment**' panels where you are invited to sign off on areas of competence or knowledge that you have mastered. These cover most of the theory, practice and good habits that you need to acquire in order to become a safe and competent driver. By signing off on these commitments, you are affirming that:

- You have mastered a particular area of competence or knowledge;
- You understand the risks and hazards relating to that competence; and
- You are making a commitment about your own behaviour as a driver.

Don't sign off on a commitment until you're fully confident that you have mastered the competence or knowledge it relates to. If you feel you're close but not quite there on a particular area, practise and repeat it until you are, or ask your sponsor or ADI for advice. For example, you can focus on that area during your next practice session. You should also ask your sponsor to 'sign off' on the commitments as a way of confirming your competence in each area. For convenience the '**My commitment**' panels are also included at the back of this book.

Competencies: things to know and things to do

To become a safe and competent driver, there are things you need to know and things you need to do:

Things you need to know	Things you need to do
The things you need to know include:	The things you need to do include:
• Rules and regulations, including the *Rules of the Road* and the rules governing the learner permit;	• Learning how to manoeuvre your car and use all its controls competently;
• Car control, safety and maintenance tasks: how the car works and the correct way to use the car's controls; car safety and maintenance tasks; and the cockpit drill;	• Practising your driving skills within a structured programme;
	• Controlling and manoeuvring the car in traffic;
• How to show consideration for vulnerable road users; and	• Learning to plan ahead, including use of maps and other navigation aids; and
• How to recognise, manage and avoid risk.	• Driving at night and in other challenging conditions.

The things you learn and the things you do go hand in hand and influence each other. The theory you learn informs how you drive; and your driving practice makes sense of the theory you have learnt. Mastering the theory and practice together helps you to develop the good habits of safe and competent driving.

Údarás Um Shábháilteacht Ar Bhóithre
Road Safety Authority

Learning in a structured way

Developing all of these skills takes time and patience. The best way to learn is within a structured environment, with the help of an approved driving instructor (ADI) and a 'sponsor'. Just like any other task, you will want the best possible coaching, to ensure that you start off on the right foot and develop good habits as you learn. Bad habits can be very hard to 'unlearn', and they also make it much more difficult to pass the driving test.

When you have developed the full range of skills to a satisfactory level, you can do the driving test and be confident that you will pass. Passing the driving test, however, does not mean that you are an expert driver – even the most 'experienced' driver can be a learner at times – for example when they're driving in challenging conditions such as those brought on by snow, fog or very heavy rain. Most insurance companies will not regard a driver as 'experienced' until they have driven over 100,000km – based on average annual driving in Ireland, that's about 6 years of driving.

Different weather conditions can totally change driving conditions.

My commitment: 1

I understand the responsibility of taking a car onto the road and of sharing the road with other people. I am ready to take on that personal responsibility and to take ownership of how I learn to drive.

Signed (Learner)   Signed (Sponsor)

Who's going to help you?

You and your Approved Driving Instructor (ADI)

While you are learning to drive a car, guidance and support from an Approved Driving Instructor (ADI) is extremely helpful. First-time learner permit holders must take the Essential Driver Training (EDT) programme with an ADI before taking the practical driving test. See www.rsa.ie for more information about who must take the EDT programme

ADIs are very experienced and have a great deal of knowledge about driving. They are also experienced at passing on their expert knowledge. If you have any questions about driving, your ADI will be able to answer them for you.

You will probably do most of your practice driving with a sponsor but it might be worth thinking about booking a lesson with an ADI for your first driving experience on a public road. Most ADIs' cars have dual controls and the instructors themselves have the skills and knowledge to make your first trip a safe learning experience.

The RSA website includes a list of all registered ADIs, sorted by county.

See www.rsa.ie/RSA/Learner-Drivers/Safe-Driving/Find-an-instructor/

You and your sponsor

Your sponsor is the person who takes responsibility for helping you to learn how to drive. This means they will help you to:

- Plan your programme of learning;
- Learn the basic skills of controlling the car;
- Develop good road sense; and
- Form good habits that will make you a safe and competent driver.

The programme of learning that your sponsor helps you with is in addition to driving instruction that you take with an ADI.

Your sponsor is a very important resource to have as you learn to drive. You will be spending quite a bit of time with your sponsor so that person should be someone you trust and respect and from whom you can accept instruction and coaching. Your sponsor must hold a full licence for two years and should have lots of driving experience.

For the sponsor

As the learner driver's sponsor, you play a key part in helping the learner to gain the knowledge, skills and good habits that will help them to become a safe and competent driver. To be a good sponsor takes time, effort and patience. At this stage, driving a car is second nature to you, and you don't have to think about how you do things. To teach the skills of driving means that you have to examine each procedure and break it down into several smaller steps.

You also need to encourage, praise and review the learner's performance. You need to avoid strong criticism or blame. Don't put the learner into situations before they are ready for them or have the skills to handle them – and don't allow the learner to control the pace of learning. The task of driving involves making decisions all the time, and one of your tasks as a sponsor is to help the learner to develop decision-making skills. Sometimes you will need to tell the learner what to do, but mostly you will be coaching them in situations where they find out for themselves. They will learn much better by doing rather than by being told what to do. As a sponsor, you need to:

- Talk with the ADI to make sure that the learner is not over-challenged;
- Start with easy tasks and gradually move on to more difficult ones; and encourage the learner to practise each skill until it has been mastered.
- Encourage the learner to set out their goals and to understand how the goals can be met within planned practice sessions. You should also try to make sure that the learner does not try to take on too much in a session;
- Give the learner plenty of notice for manoeuvres or turns that you want them to take;
- Be alert and ready to take over in the event of the learner getting into difficulty;
- Review the practice session – ask the learner to talk through the drive they did. For example, you could ask 'were you happy with the way you dealt with the roundabouts?';
- Try to instil in the learner the importance of observation, judgement, planning and reaction skills. Don't just focus on car control skills; and
- Take into account and make use of the learner's previous road experience – for example, as a cyclist.

As well as teaching the learner the skills of driving, you'll also be coaching them in how to share the road with other people in a responsible, courteous and safe way.

Throughout this book there are notes and tips that are intended to help the sponsor.

For the sponsor	I am willing to act as a sponsor for [ ] who wants to learn how to drive. I understand the responsibilities I am taking on and will work with [ ] to help him or her become a safe, competent and responsible driver.
Signed	

Who should you choose as your sponsor?

Usually, the sponsor is a family member such as a parent, or an aunt or uncle. If you want, you could also have more than one sponsor, depending on their availability to accompany you on your practice journeys. A good sponsor is someone who:

- Has experience as a driver and has had a full car licence for at least two years;
- Has the ability to explain and teach the skills of driving and to coach you as you learn and practise those skills;
- Has an understanding of the problems that learner drivers face;
- Can stay calm and patient under pressure;
- Accepts the responsibility of taking part in your learning; and
- Can devote a good deal of time and effort to the task – and do it without any payment. Only approved driving instructors (ADIs) may accept money or reward for driving instruction

When you are taking driving lessons with an approved driving instructor, you should consider asking your sponsor to accompany you on a lesson.

Stages in learning to drive

When you're learning to drive, you progress through several different stages. All the time you're adding to your knowledge, growing in competence, and developing good habits. For most learners, these stages can be summarised as follows:

Stage	Description
1. First steps	At the beginning you have to take in a lot of new information and develop new skills. When you are driving, you have to keep all this information in your head, to pick out the bits that are relevant at a particular time, and to apply that information to the task in hand. This can be hard, and you should not expect to achieve too much too quickly.
2. Developing skills and gaining experience	At this stage you still have to go through the same process of selecting information, but you will be getting better at knowing what is relevant in any situation, and you'll be getting more comfortable with the skills needed.
3. Mastering skills and acquiring confidence	By now, figuring out what to do in any situation will become almost automatic. You will be reacting appropriately to situations as they arise without seeming to think about them.

My commitment: 2
I am willing to learn how to drive in a structured and controlled way with the help of my sponsor and my ADI.

Signed (Learner)	Signed (Sponsor)

What you need to progress

The right information, the right coaching and the right experience will help you to develop your confidence on the road, but not too much. A good driver is a confident driver; but an over-confident driver might not always judge situations accurately.

The learner driver and the law

Before you drive a car on the public road, you need to make sure that you are legal in every way:

- Your vehicle must be insured and you must be insured to drive it;
- Your vehicle must be taxed and NCT-certified (if necessary);
- You must have an up-to-date learner permit – see **Getting your learner permit** on page 17;
- While you are learning you must be accompanied at all times by a suitable qualified driver; and
- Your car must display regulation L-plates (front and rear) at all times while you are driving – one of the advantages of displaying L-plates is that other drivers may be more considerate towards you if they know you are a learner.

Staying safe

Get into the habit of 'thinking safe' at all times.

- Always wear your seatbelt, and make sure that all your passengers wear theirs too.
- Don't ever drive while under the influence of alcohol or drugs (legal or illegal). If you are convicted of a drink driving offence, you will be automatically disqualified from driving for a minimum of three months, and you could face a jail sentence if you are involved in a serious collision. If you are on prescribed medication, ask your doctor if this is likely to affect your driving.
- Don't use your mobile phone while driving. Not only is it illegal, but learning to drive requires your total concentration. The last thing you need is the distraction of talking or texting on a mobile while you are practising.
- You need to be fully alert when you are driving, so don't drive when you are very tired. Tiredness is a factor in many collisions.

The aim of the *Rules of the Road* is to promote safety, good driving practice and courtesy in using our roads in accordance with the law. It is an interpretation of the law from a road safety point of view.

Always keep a copy of the *Rules of the Road* handy, so that you can check up on any point you're not clear about.

Getting your learner permit

Before you can get a learner permit, you must pass a theory test. See www.theorytest.ie for more information on how to apply for the theory test.

- Application forms for learner permits are available at Garda stations, Motor Tax Offices and public libraries.
- You must be at least 17 years old to apply for a learner permit for a car or light van (category B), and you must be normally resident in Ireland.
- The first time you apply for a learner permit you must supply a satisfactory eyesight report. This report must be completed by a registered ophthalmic optician or by a registered medical practitioner.
- A learner permit is normally valid for two years from the date of issue. You can apply to do the car driving test when you get your first learner permit. However, you may not sit your driving test until you have held a category B learner permit for at least six months. See **www.rsa.ie** for information on those who must complete a programme of Essential Driver Training.

See also

The *Rules of the Road* includes more detailed information about getting a learner permit.

My commitment: 3

I understand the legal issues relating to driving a car and I commit myself to safe and responsible practice.

Signed (Learner)

Signed (Sponsor)

2. Controls and manoeuvring the car

In this chapter

This chapter helps you to start learning the basic skills you need to control and manoeuvre a car. It covers the following:

- Basic car maintenance knowledge: you need some basic knowledge of car maintenance before you learn to drive, as it is part of your responsibility as a driver to ensure that your car is safe and roadworthy;
- Getting to know your car: this includes the basic safety checks or 'cockpit drill' that you do when you sit into the driver's seat. You need to be familiar with all of the car's controls – you need to know where they are and how to operate them.
- Information on starting and stopping for the first time: this can be quite nerve-racking, but your ADI or sponsor will ensure that you do this in a safe traffic-free environment.
- Information about basic controls: as you learn to start and stop, you need to learn the basic controls of the accelerator, clutch and brakes, and you need to learn how to steer the car. Again, your ADI or sponsor will be there to make sure that your learning experience is safe and rewarding.
- Information about your first time on the road.

By the end of this chapter you will be driving. You will have learnt the basic skills of controlling and manoeuvring the car in a safe and competent manner, and you will be putting into practice much of the theory you have learned. You will also begin to understand what it takes to share the road with other people.

Basic car knowledge

At this stage you're probably impatient to get behind the wheel and get started. Before you do, however, you need to have some basic car knowledge. You are about to learn how to control a very powerful and potentially dangerous piece of equipment, and you are responsible for making sure that the car you drive is in a safe and roadworthy condition. In particular, you need to make sure that you have enough fuel, that your tyres are correctly inflated (tyre pressure) and that your lights are working correctly. During your Essential Driver Training, your ADI will help you learn the pre-start checks that you need to carry out.

Familiarise yourself with your car's user manual. If you own the car, you are responsible for making sure that it is properly and regularly serviced.

Fuel

The one basic maintenance task that you will have do regularly is to put fuel in your car. Ask your sponsor to show you how to fill up the fuel tank at the service station. Petrol is highly flammable, so be very careful when you're filling up. You also need to know:

- How to check the fuel gauge to see that you have enough fuel;
- Where the fuel tank is on your car and how to open the cap – the fuel cap is usually at the back of the car, on the left or right side depending on the make and model; and
- Whether your car takes petrol or diesel – putting the wrong fuel in your car could seriously damage the engine.

Tyres: tread depth and pressure

Well maintained tyres are essential for safety. Check the tyres and look for any defects such as bubbles or blistering in the tyre walls or any other visible defects. As a minimum, tyres should have a tread depth of 1.6mm. Bald or unevenly worn tyres are very dangerous – your stopping distance is much greater and you are much more likely to skid. For safety reasons, many drivers replace their tyres before the tread gets as low as the legal minimum.

Maintaining your tyres at the correct pressure is very important for safe, economical driving. You should check the tyre pressure regularly – at least once a month and more regularly (even daily) if you drive a lot.

Your car's user manual will tell you what the correct pressure is for your car. Ask your sponsor to show you how to perform this simple check. Don't forget to check the spare tyre.

For some cars the recommended tyre pressure is different for front and rear tyres.

Horn

Your horn is an essential safety device. Every now and then, check that it's working.

Lights

You need to check that all your lights are working properly. Ask someone to help you with this – get them to stand outside the car and to check that the lights come on when you turn them on. You need to check all the following lights:

- Main headlights (full and dipped)
- Number plate lights
- Indicators (front and rear; left and right)
- Fog lights, front and rear (where fitted)
- Side lights (front and rear)
- Brake lights
- Reversing lights

See your car's user manual for instructions on how to change the light bulbs.

Under the bonnet

First find the bonnet release lever. Check your car's manual or ask your sponsor to help you find it if you are not sure where it is. With the bonnet open, identify the following:

- **The oil dipstick** – you need to know where this is to check the oil level in your car. Engine oil is essential to keep your engine lubricated and running smoothly. You will need to check the oil every now and then. See the car's user manual for help with this.

- **Windscreen washer fluid reservoir** – this is a container that holds the water you use to wash the windscreen. Keep this topped up. There are also some cleaning fluids you can buy that can be used on their own or diluted with water.

- **Coolant level** – the coolant is a mixture of water and anti-freeze fluid that helps to keep your engine cool. It is usually stored in a reservoir towards the front of the engine. The level of coolant should be above the marked 'min' level (minimum level). If it is not, you need to top it up with coolant. Never open the reservoir cap when the engine is hot. Let the engine cool before you add any coolant, and don't fill it above the 'max' level (maximum level).

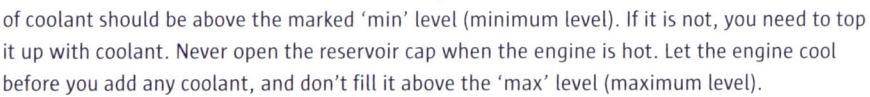

My commitment: 4

I understand how important it is to maintain my car in a safe and roadworthy condition. I have a good understanding of the basic service and maintenance requirements of my car, and I know how to carry out basic checks myself.

Signed (Learner)   Signed (Sponsor)

Know your car – before you turn on the engine

Before you turn on the engine and begin to drive your car, there are a few things you need to know and a few things you need to be able to do.

Getting in and out of the car

Each time you get in or out of a car, you need to make sure that it is safe to do so. A car door opening can be a hazard to passing traffic, particularly to cyclists. You are also responsible for making sure that your passengers open their doors only when it is safe to do so.

Make yourself comfortable

The first thing you need to do when you sit into a car and before you turn on the engine is to check that the door is closed properly. Then make sure you're comfortable – adjust the driver's seat if you need to. Make sure that you have good visibility and that you can reach the pedals, the steering wheel and all the hand controls easily. The driver's seat can usually be moved up and down and back and forth, and you can also adjust the angle of the back of the seat. In most cars you can also adjust the angle of the steering wheel.

Make sure you can let in the clutch fully with your left foot without having to stretch, and that you can move your right foot easily between the accelerator and the brake.

Ask your driving instructor or your sponsor to check the position of your feet as you control the pedals. Not everyone is comfortable in the same position, so as you become more experienced, you will find the position that suits you best.

Check that the head restraint on your seat is in the correct position.

- The top of the head restraint should be in line with the top of the head.
- The centre of the head restraint should be roughly in line with the top of the ears.

Study the controls

When you are driving you need to use the car's controls without having to look for them, so you should be totally familiar with them (where they are and how to use them) before you go on the road. Without turning on the engine:

- Practise letting the clutch in and out (very slowly and smoothly) and changing up and down through the gears;
- Practise moving your right foot from the accelerator to the brake and back again;
- If you are on level ground, practise engaging and disengaging the handbrake (parking brake) – you can secure the car with the foot brake to stop it moving back or forwards; and
- Check the location of the various controls, including the indicators, horn, wipers, climate control, demisters, and lights – side lights and headlights (dipped and full).

Consult your car's user manual for a full description of all the controls.

Advanced controls

Many modern cars have advanced technological control systems that are designed to improve car safety or help the driver in various ways. These include systems such as:

- Advanced driver assistance systems (ADAS);
- Anti-lock braking systems (ABS);
- Electronic stability programmes; and
- Lane departure warning systems.

If your car has advanced technological controls, make sure to learn how to use them, and make sure you know what they can and can't do. You also need to be aware that some of these systems can improve a car's safety, but they in no way reduce the need for you to stay alert to all possible hazards while on the road.

Adjust your mirrors

Adjust the internal mirror and the external mirrors so that you have the best possible view of what is happening behind and to the side of the car.

The central mirror should enable you to see most or all of the back window. Make sure there is no luggage or other objects blocking your rear view. The side mirrors help you see behind you along the sides of your car.

Practice tip

Cockpit drill

Get into the habit of performing a 'cockpit drill' every time you sit into the driver's seat of a car. This is a basic safety and comfort check that you should do before you move off. Check that:

- The bonnet and the boot or hatchback door are closed;
- All doors are safely closed;
- Your seat is at a comfortable height and angle and you can reach the pedals and all of the controls easily.
- The mirrors are correctly adjusted and clean;
- The handbrake is on and the car is in neutral;
- Everybody is wearing a seatbelt; and
- The head restraint is properly adjusted.

Checking blind spots

Be aware that there are 'blind spots' to the front, rear and sides of your car. There will be times when you will need to look over your shoulder as well as in the mirrors.

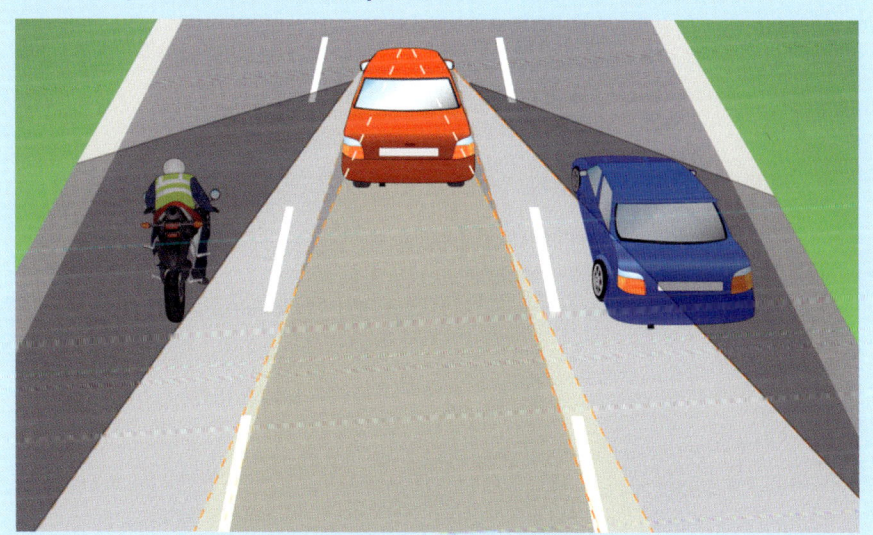

In this picture of a three-lane carriageway, the driver of the red car can see a part of the blue car in the right side mirror; but the motorcycle in the inside lane is entirely 'hidden' in a blind spot.

For the sponsor

Additional mirror

As an extra safety feature, consider fitting a passenger-side rear view mirror so that you can see behind without turning around These are usually suction-cup mounted and can be easily fitted and removed.

My commitment: 5

I know what to do when I first sit into the driver's seat of a car. I can operate all the manual controls without taking my eyes off the road.

Signed (Learner)   Signed (Sponsor)

Starting and stopping the car: the first time

Up to now, you've been gaining knowledge about your car and about driving. Now it's time to actually begin to do something, to start the car, move off and then stop the car.

Moving off is probably the most difficult manoeuvre that you will learn. You need to learn to control the clutch by slowly releasing it while at the same time putting gentle pressure on the accelerator.

For the sponsor

Choosing the location and the conditions

The location you choose to teach the learner how to start and stop the car for the first time is very important. Examples of suitable locations include empty car parks, disused roads, or other places where you will not meet any pedestrians, traffic or obstructions. The ground should be level so that at this stage the learner doesn't have to worry about the hand-brake. Choose a day when the weather is reasonably fine and visibility is good.

Starting the engine

Before you turn the key in the ignition, check that the parking brake (or handbrake) is **on** and that the gear lever is in neutral.

For most cars, you turn the key clockwise and allow it to spring back when the engine starts running. This should take no more than a second or so.

If your car has a different starting mechanism (such as a **Start** button) and you are not sure how to use it, ask your sponsor to show you how it works.

You need to get to know the sound of the engine. So, with the gear lever still in neutral, gently press the accelerator once or twice so you can hear the change in the engine sound.

Moving off and stopping

Moving off and stopping for the first time is not easy, and the only way you'll learn it is to do it. The following steps tell you how it works in theory – for the practice, it's over to you. Not many people get it absolutely right the first time.

Your sponsor will ensure that you are in a safe location and that you can do no harm, to yourself or anyone else or to the car. Make sure the parking brake (or handbrake) is **on** before you start.

1.	Press the clutch down fully with your left foot and hold it there, and put the gear lever into first gear.
2.	Release the handbrake – as long as you are on level ground, you won't roll back or forward.
3.	Very gradually let the clutch pedal up with your left foot while at the same time pressing gently on the accelerator with your right foot.
4.	As the car begins to move forward, let the clutch fully up and gently increase the pressure on the accelerator. The car will now move forward slowly. For the moment, leave your left foot hovering above the clutch.
5.	To stop the car, take your right foot off the accelerator and gently press down on the brake. Press in the clutch with your left foot before you come to a complete stop – this stops the engine from cutting out.
6.	With the clutch fully pressed in, return the gear lever to neutral and apply the parking brake or handbrake.

Well done! You have now started the car, moved a short distance and stopped. You now need to *practise and repeat* this manoeuvre over and over until it becomes second nature to you. You'll probably cut out a few times as you're learning, but don't worry – you'll soon get the hang of it.

Údarás Um Shábháilteacht Ar Bhóithre
Road Safety Authority

Moving off from the kerb

As you practise starting and moving off, get into the habit of checking your mirror, signalling and checking your blind spots before you actually move off. This is the **Mirror–Signal–Mirror (blind spots)–Manoeuvre** routine.

Mirror
Look in your rear-view and side mirrors to check that it is safe to move out.

Signal
Signal your intention to move by turning on an indicator.

Mirror (and check blind spots)
Check your mirror again and check your blind spots by looking over your shoulder.

Manoeuvre
Begin the manoeuvre.

Steering the car

You use the steering wheel to control the direction you want the car to go in. As you are practising moving off and driving short distances, get used to the feel of the steering wheel and how the car responds to the steering adjustments you make. Don't worry if you understeer or oversteer at the beginning. You'll soon be able to make very exact adjustments in the steering. Practise steering the car to very precise points.

Hold the steering wheel with both hands, firmly but not too tightly. The position of your hands on the wheel should be comfortable and give you most control – the 'ten-to-two' position suits most people, as in the 'Manoeuvre' picture on page 26. You also need to get used to steering with just your right hand – while you change gears with your left.

Most cars now have power-assisted steering and don't require much physical effort.

Avoid turning the steering wheel while the car is stationary, as this causes wear on the tyres and can damage the steering mechanism.

My commitment: 6
I am able to start the car, drive a few metres and stop the car in a safe, traffic-free location.
Signed (Learner)   Signed (Sponsor)

Changing up to second gear ...

You use first gear when you are moving off. As you increase your speed you change up through the gears.

Second and third gears are intermediate gears and you use them in slower-moving traffic or while climbing hills.

On open roads, you will normally drive drive in the highest gear possible.

Once you are reasonably well practised at starting, moving off and stopping, you can learn how to change up to second gear. Follow these steps:

1.	Ease your foot off the accelerator, and at the same time press the clutch down fully with your left foot and put the gear lever into second gear.
2.	Very gradually let the clutch pedal up with your left foot while at the same time pressing gently on the accelerator. Listen to how the engine sound changes when you change gear.

... and to third gear

To change up to third gear, you follow the same steps as for changing into second, except that you put the gear lever into the third gear position. You can do this later when you are driving on the open road.

My commitment: 7
I am able to drive the car in a traffic-free location and can change gears.
Signed (Learner)   Signed (Sponsor)

Braking

How hard you press the brake determines how quickly the car will slow down and stop.

In the normal course of driving, you should aim to brake early and progressively. In other words, don't wait until just before you need to stop to put your foot on the brake – slow down in advance by pressing gently on the brake, and then pressing more firmly to come to a complete stop. This will give you and your passengers a smoother drive. Also, it's easier on the car, and will save you fuel.

You also need to take into account that a loaded vehicle (for example, one with five people – driver and four passengers) takes a longer distance to stop.

Practice tip

There will, however, be situations where you need to brake very quickly. For that reason, you should begin to practise braking quickly at low speeds in a safe traffic-free environment.

For the sponsor

Braking practice

You need to be sure that the learner has mastered the basics of braking while still practising in a safe traffic-free environment. This includes:

- **Normal, 'progressive' braking**: help the learner to brake very smoothly and evenly; and

- **Quick reaction, 'emergency' braking**: help the learner to practise quick reaction braking by giving some kind of agreed signal (verbal or visual) so that they can get the feel of what it's like to have to stop very quickly. For example, say 'When I say the word "stop" bring the car to a complete stop as quickly as you can.'

Your first time on the road

Up to now you have driven in very safe traffic-free locations. You have mastered the skills of starting and stopping the car and changing gears. You are now ready to drive on the public road for the first time, in light traffic.

For the sponsor

Planning the learner's first road trip

In the early stages of learning, the learner should drive only in very light traffic, in daylight, in good weather, and on fairly level wide roads with good visibility.

Combining knowledge and practice

The first time you drive on the public road you need to bring together all the knowledge you have gained and put it into practice. That's not as easy as it sounds. You're probably still getting used to using the car's controls and there is so much information about the road environment to take in, remember and act upon.

The first time you are on the road, there are three main areas you need to concentrate on:

1.	Controlling the car and its position on the road.
2.	Reading the road signs and understanding how they apply to you as a driver. You must obey signs that tell you to do something – for example, Stop signs, No Entry signs and so on.
3.	Observing and anticipating what other road users are doing; and giving them advance warning of what you are going to do.

On the public road

While you are driving on the public road, you need to:

- Maintain a speed that suits your own capabilities, the traffic and road conditions;
- Scan the road ahead and to the sides at all times, and also keep an eye in your mirrors to check what's coming behind you; and
- Check your mirrors and signal before you make manoeuvres such as changing lane or turning at a junction.

My commitment: 8
I am able to drive the car on the public road in a quiet location in very light traffic.

Signed (Learner)	Signed (Sponsor)

For the sponsor

Providing a commentary

Get the learner to 'comment' on what's happening on the road and to point out any likely sources of danger as a way of actively observing what's happening on the road. Here are some examples:

> 'The red car ahead is signalling that it is turning right at the next junction.'
>
> 'That bus is about to pull out.'
>
> 'On the pavement, a boy is bouncing a ball.'
>
> 'A pedestrian has pushed the button at the traffic lights ahead. I will have to stop if the lights change before I get there.'

The purpose of this exercise is to improve the learner's skills of observation, anticipation and judgement, and to enable you to assess their progress.

Practice tip

The RSA recommends the use of daytime running lights (where fitted) or dipped headlights during daylight.

3. Gaining experience on the road

In this chapter

By now you have learned the basic skills of driving, and guess what? – you're a driver. But you're not yet as skilled or experienced as you need to be. The road conditions you've met and the type of journeys you've made are quite limited. Now you need to extend the range of your road experience by taking on more challenging tasks and more varied journeys. You can do this with the guidance of your sponsor.

This chapter aims to help you and your sponsor to plan practice journeys so that you can meet a variety of different challenges in the course of your driving practice. You will already be familiar with the theory of many of these challenges from your knowledge of the *Rules of the Road*. Now it's time to learn as a driver how to safely negotiate junctions and roundabouts, how to deal with obstructions, how to make sure that you are in the right lane, how to drive at an appropriate speed and to keep an appropriate distance from the vehicle in front, and so on.

This chapter also describes how you can extend your driving skills to take in tasks such as starting on a hill, parking, reversing, and practising emergency stops.

Once you have passed your test and gained your full licence, you can drive on motorways – this chapter describes some of the challenges you will face in motorway driving.

Planning practice journeys

During the course of instruction from your ADI or as part of Essential Driver Training, you will be driving under the supervision of an ADI and gaining experience of different types of road and road conditions. As well as driving with your instructor, you should also spend time practising your driving while accompanied by your sponsor. Your first few practice journeys with your sponsor should be in daylight, in good weather, on quiet roads and at a time when traffic is light. With the help of your sponsor, you need to gradually take on more challenging journeys. Plan to have at least one practice journey a week; and over the course of a number of weeks, your practice journeys should include all of the following:

- Turning onto and off main roads
- Negotiating roundabouts
- Reversing
- Overtaking a slow-moving vehicle
- Changing lanes
- Starting on a hill
- Parking in a car park
- Stopping and moving off at traffic lights

Every practice journey you plan can give you valuable experience and present new challenges. Include a mix of urban, suburban and rural driving in your plan. Build your practice journeys into your routine – for example, a trip to a supermarket, to a cinema or to a sports event could be the basis of your practice session. Use a map to help you to plan your practice journeys.

Practice tip

After each practice journey, review the challenges you faced, and identify the manoeuvres you need to practise more. Sign off on the commitments as you become competent at particular tasks and feel confident dealing with particular situations. Make sure your sponsor agrees with your own assessment.

For the sponsor

Planning variety in practice routes

Plan the route for each practice journey in advance, and talk to the learner about the challenges that the journey will involve. For example, a typical journey to a supermarket might include:

- Driving on a dual carriageway – this could be a opportunity to give advice about lane discipline;
- Turning right at traffic lights – the learner will need to move into the right lane at the appropriate time;
- Driving through an urban one-way system, with turning arrows marked on the road;
- Stopping for pedestrians at a pedestrian crossing;
- Waiting at a yellow box junction; and
- Reversing into a parking space.

Before setting off, review the sections in the *Rules of the Road* relevant to the new challenges and tasks that the learner will meet.

My commitment: 9

I understand the importance of planning my practice journeys in advance and reviewing them afterwards with my sponsor.

Signed (Learner)	Signed (Sponsor)

Reading the road

As you drive along any road you are receiving information all the time. You need to be able to take in this information and respond appropriately. You already know what the road signs mean from the *Rules of the Road*, but it's not always easy for learners to concentrate on driving safely and reading the road as they go.

Scan the road as you drive, and get into the habit of observing all of the information that road markings and road signs give you. Remember to observe the *Rules of the Road* and to follow all traffic controls at all times. Be particularly alert for any hazards that arise as you drive. It will soon become second nature for you to take in and process all the information you receive.

Road markings	Markings painted on the road surface give you a lot of complex information – for example, a solid white line in the centre of the road tells you that all traffic must keep to the left of the line (except in an emergency or for access), and a double yellow line at the side of the road tells you that you may not park there at any time.
	Also painted on the road surface are traffic lane indications and arrows, bus lane markers, cycle lane markers and direction arrows.
Yellow box junctions	You must not enter a yellow box junction unless you can clear it without stopping. An exception is when you want to turn right – in this case you may enter the box while waiting for traffic coming from the opposite direction. However, you should not enter the box if it means you would block other traffic that has the right of way.
Regulatory and warning signs	Posted on the side of the road or above the road there are regulatory signs that you must obey. These include speed limits, 'Stop' and 'Yield' signs and 'No Parking' signs. Also posted along the side of the road are warning signs that tell you about junctions ahead, sharp bends, road works, and other potential hazards.
Traffic lights	You must obey all traffic lights. Where two or more sets of traffic lights are a short distance apart, be particularly careful to obey those closest to you.
Direction signs	Direction signs point the way to different places – these are found, for example, coming up to junctions and at junctions.

Learn how to distinguish between information that is relevant and information that is not relevant to you. For example, if you are driving to Ballina, you might know that the turn off you need is coming up soon, so you'll be alert for signs for Ballina and can usually ignore signs for other destinations.

Practice tip

In the early stages of learning, drive in locations that you know so that you won't have to worry too much about direction signs or getting lost in an unfamiliar area.

For the sponsor

Learner's knowledge of road signs and markings

Test the learner on various road signs and markings as you meet them. Be careful, however, not to distract the learner when they are dealing with a complex situation.

Knowing the *Rules of the Road* book and interpreting them correctly takes time and the learner will need help from the ADI and from you as the sponsor.

My commitment: 10

I am able to 'read the road' – to take in the information I need from road markings, regulatory and warning signs, traffic lights, and direction signs.

Signed (Learner)   Signed (Sponsor)

Knowing your position on the road

Knowing your position on the road and being able to steer accurately and precisely are important skills. Learning them will help you become a competent driver and help you to share the road safely with other road users.

In the early stages of practice, learner drivers often have difficulty 'visualising' (seeing in your mind's eye) where the four wheels of the car are on the road. You will need to be able to know or visualise where the front and back of the car are in relation to other vehicles and road 'furniture' (for example, bollards), and where the sides of the car are in relation to the kerb and lane markings.

Where lanes are not marked	Where lanes are marked
Keep to the left as you drive, but not too close to the verge or to parked cars or the pavement (in urban areas). In wet weather avoid splashing pedestrians or cyclists.	Position your car centrally between the lane markers. If you need to change lanes, follow the **Mirror – Signal – Mirror (blind spots) – Manoeuvre** routine. If you are going to turn off to the left or right, plan ahead so that you are in the correct lane when you arrive at the junction.

Practice tip — Observing the position of cars ahead and behind you will give a sense of where you should be on the road.

Keep your distance

Don't drive too close to the car in front of you. The faster the traffic is moving, the greater the distance you should allow. Keep a safe headway by ensuring you are at least two seconds behind the vehicle in front. This is known as the two second rule.

The distance it will take you to stop in an emergency depends on many things, including how alert you are, the type and condition of the road surface, and how good your brakes and tyres are. Remember that a loaded vehicle takes a longer distance to stop.

The *Rules of the Road* sets out the minimum stopping distances for different speeds and road conditions.

Never 'tailgate' the car in front of you. If that car brakes suddenly, you may be unable to avoid colliding with it. You should leave a greater distance to the front if there is a car very close behind trying to overtake you – this will make it easier for the car behind you to overtake and then return to the left-hand lane. It will also reduce the risks associated with the overtaking driver's behaviour.

For the sponsor

The two-second rule

The two-second rule gives a rough guide by which a driver can judge if the distance to the vehicle in front is enough.

Explain this to the learner, and help pick out landmarks to use as stopping 'targets'. The learner can practise measuring stopping distances in this way.

See the *Rules of the Road* for more information on the two-second rule.

Lanes at junctions

At many junctions, road markings indicate the lanes for turning left or right or going straight. Keep to the lane for the direction you want to go in. Be particularly careful where a lane has two directional arrows – drivers in that lane might do something that you are not expecting.

Lanes on a dual carriageway

The right-hand lane on a dual carriageway or motorway is for overtaking slower-moving vehicles: it is not the 'fast lane'. Once you have overtaken the slow-moving vehicle, move back into the left lane, unless you intend overtaking another vehicle a short distance ahead.

Lanes on one-way streets

One-way streets can be confusing when you first meet them. For example, you might find yourself in a centre lane with lines of cars passing you on both sides. Follow the road marking for the direction you wish to take, and drive within the lane markers. Use the mirror–signal–mirror–manoeuvre routine when you want to change lanes.

My commitment: 11
I know how to position my car on the road. I keep a safe distance between my car and the vehicle ahead; I understand how lanes work and can position my car in the appropriate lane at all times while driving.

Signed (Learner)   Signed (Sponsor)

Dealing with junctions

Junctions come in all shapes and sizes. Some are simple T-junctions that join country lanes to small country roads; others are busier junctions in towns (with traffic lights) and join two or more roads. Motorway interchanges are more complex, with ramped access and exit roads. Junctions are where different streams of traffic meet, and pedestrians are more likely to cross the road at a junction than anywhere else. You need to be extra careful at junctions for these reasons.

In the course of your driving practice, you should try to meet as many different kinds of junction as possible. The manoeuvres you perform should include making left and right turns, driving straight through, using filter lanes, turning at box junctions, entering and exiting roundabouts, and so on.

The *Rules of the Road* gives comprehensive guidance on how you should approach and drive at junctions.

Stop or yield?

At most junctions the road priority is clearly indicated, and the point at which the minor road joins the major road normally shows a STOP or YIELD sign.

STOP sign
Always stop when you come to a STOP sign (even if you can see no traffic on the major road), and yield to traffic that has the right of way.

YIELD sign
Always slow down and prepare to stop as you approach a YIELD sign. You must yield to traffic that has the right of way.

For the sponsor

The right of way

Explain the various right of way rules to the learner. The *Rules of the Road* gives detailed information about the right of way – see under Junctions and Roundabouts.

Driving on a major road

When you are driving on a major road, you have priority over traffic emerging from minor roads. Signs that tell you about junctions ahead are for your information – they're not telling you to do anything, except to be careful and to be aware that cars and other traffic may be waiting to join the main road or to turn off onto the minor road.

Don't overtake in advance of a junction. A driver turning left from a side road to the right might not have checked traffic coming from their left – see the picture on page 39.

Turning off a major road at a junction

Turning left	
	O Check your mirror and signal in advance. Adjust your position and slow down as you approach the junction. Where possible, move closer to the left side of the road or into the left turning lane (where there is one). Be very careful if you have to cross in front of a bus lane to turn left.
	O Give way to any pedestrians already crossing the minor road.
	O Don't cut across cyclists who are going straight ahead on the major road.
	O Keep to the left-hand side of the road you are joining, without swinging out over the area where cars might be waiting to emerge onto the main road

Turning right

- Check your mirrors and signal in advance. Adjust your position and slow down as you approach the junction. Where possible, move closer to the left centre of the road to enable traffic going straight on to pass you on the inside; or use the turning lane where this is provided.
- If necessary, stop and wait until there is a safe gap in oncoming traffic before turning into the minor road. In this situation it is very important not to begin to steer the wheels until you start to move.
- Before you make the turn, check your mirrors again for traffic coming from behind – in particular, for any traffic that could be trying to overtake you.
- Make sure there is nothing blocking your entry into the minor road that could leave you in an exposed position on the major road.
- Give way to any pedestrians already crossing the minor road.

In this case, car A is positioned just to the left of the centre of the road. It is waiting to turn right, and has left enough space for car B to pass on the left-hand side.

Practice tip — The speed appropriate to the minor road you are joining might be considerably less than the speed you've been driving at on the major road.

Údarás Um Shábháilteacht Ar Bhóithre
Road Safety Authority

Joining a major road at a junction

When you approach a major road from a minor road, make sure that you stop or yield as required by the roadside sign. If there are no signs, wait at the entrance to the junction until the road is clear. Be extra careful before joining a major road – traffic on the major road is likely to be travelling quite fast.

- Check your mirror and signal in advance. Adjust your position and slow down as you approach the junction.
- Your sight lines might not be very good as you emerge from the minor road, so look both ways before you join the major road. For example, in rural areas there could be bends or dips in the roadway or overhanging bushes that could affect your view. In towns or cities, parked cars, goods vehicles or buses setting down or taking on passengers could affect your view. Also, a slow-moving bus or lorry could hide a car that is about to overtake it.
- After you have joined the major road, accelerate to the speed appropriate for that road, but pay attention to the speed limits, traffic and other hazards on that road.

Always look both ways – even if you are turning left. An overtaking car coming from the left could be in the road space that you will be in after you make the turn. Also, a pedestrian might be crossing the main road.

Slip roads

Slip roads are designed to make it easy to join and leave major roads, including motorways and dual carriageways.

Joining a major road	Signal your intention to join the main road and give way to traffic already on it. Your speed should be close to that of traffic already on the main road, but not over the speed limit.
Leaving a major road	Move into the correct lane well in advance of the slip road and signal your intention to leave the main road.

39

Junctions with traffic lights

Some junctions with traffic lights are simple; others are complex. Before you proceed through a green light, be sure that it applies to you. For example, at complex junctions, a green arrow light might apply to traffic going straight on, but not to traffic turning left or right.

If a traffic light has been green for quite a while as you approach it, be prepared to stop when it turns amber.

You must wait at the edge of the yellow box junction until you are sure that you can clear the junction – even if you have a green light. If you are turning right, you may enter the yellow box junction and wait until it is safe to make the turn – provided that you are only prevented from turning by the traffic coming towards you.

Roundabouts

A roundabout is a kind of junction where traffic moves around a central 'island'. The advantage of roundabouts over other types of junction is that traffic flows more smoothly. For the learner, roundabouts can be quite confusing. Remember the following points:

- You need to check the direction signs more carefully than usual – your exit might not be 'obvious'.
- You need to get into the correct lane depending on which exit you are taking. If you miss your exit on a roundabout, just go around again.
- It can be difficult to see across the roundabout to where you want to go – this is particularly the case with big roundabouts that have many exits.
- You can lose your sense of direction (or orientation) as you go around;
- You might need to cross lanes (from right to left) to get to the exit you want – while at the same time other drivers may be trying to cross in the opposite direction (from left to right).
- As with other busy junctions, there might be pedestrians crossing.
- You might not have to stop as you approach a roundabout, but you must yield to traffic already on the roundabout and traffic coming from the right.

See also

Using roundabouts

For more information on roundabouts, see the video Using roundabouts on the RSA website. To locate the video, type **roundabouts** in the Search box on the home page and then click on **Search**.

Údarás Um Shábháilteacht Ar Bhóithre
Road Safety Authority

Reading the direction signs at roundabouts

Roundabouts are usually well sign-posted – both with an advance sign and signs at each exit. The advance sign shows the layout of the roundabout and where each exit leads to. You need to take note of which exit is the one you want – first, second, third and so on. This will help you plan your approach to the roundabout and help you take the exit you need.

Be alert to other drivers' signals when you are on a roundabout. Be prepared that other drivers might cross in front of you when changing lanes to get to an exit.

Seantrabh SANTRY ↑ R 132 / M50 ←→ ✈ / Áth Cliath DUBLIN / Áerfort Átha Cliath DUBLIN AIRPORT	In this example, drivers seeing this sign would take the second exit to go to Santry.
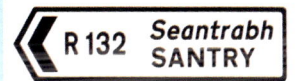 ◄ R 132 Seantrabh SANTRY	On the roundabout, each exit is usually marked clearly.

41

Exiting to the left	If your exit is to the left (9 o'clock), approach the roundabout in the left-hand lane (where there is one) and signal 'left' until you have passed through the roundabout.
Exiting straight ahead	If your exit is straight ahead (12 o'clock), approach the roundabout in the left-hand lane (where there is one) and signal 'left' after you have cleared the exit before the one you want.
Exiting to the right	If your exit is to the right (3 o'clock), approach the roundabout in the right-hand lane (where there is one), and indicate right. On a multiple-lane roundabout you may need to cross into the left-hand lane. Signal to exit (left) after you have cleared the previous exit. Make sure you follow the Mirrors – Signal – Mirrors (blind spots) – Manoeuvre routine.

My commitment: 12

I can safely negotiate all types of road junction – including left and right turns (from major to minor and from minor to major roads), slip roads, junctions with traffic lights, and roundabouts.

Signed (Learner)

Signed (Sponsor)

Controlling your speed

Excessive speed is a contributory factor in many collisions. The *Rules of the Road* sets out the maximum speed at which you may travel on different types of road.

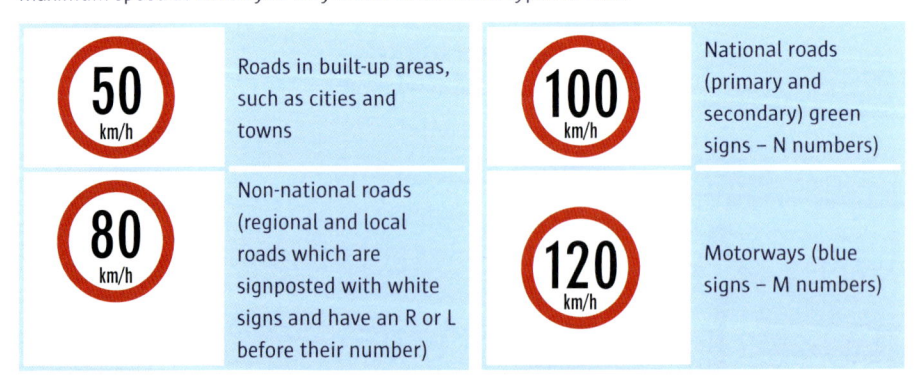

50 km/h	Roads in built-up areas, such as cities and towns	**100** km/h	National roads (primary and secondary) green signs – N numbers)
80 km/h	Non-national roads (regional and local roads which are signposted with white signs and have an R or L before their number)	**120** km/h	Motorways (blue signs – M numbers)

These are the maximum speeds allowed on these roads. They are **not** target speeds that you should try to reach. In addition to the general rules that apply, there are local variations indicated by signs posted along the roadside. These can be temporary (for example, where there are road works), or permanent (at places where the local authority has imposed a speed limit for safety reasons, for example, in an area near a school).

Within the speed limits, travel at a speed that will allow you to stop within the distance you can see to be clear. Drive at a speed you are comfortable with, and don't feel pressurised by other drivers into going faster than you want to. You should, however, try to keep up with the general flow of traffic and not travel so slowly that you could become a hazard for other road users.

Driving at an even, moderate speed

On the open road, drive at an even speed – don't speed up and slow down for no reason, and avoid having to brake suddenly in the normal course of driving.

Moderate your speed in bad weather conditions or if there are a lot of pedestrians around or if the road is very narrow.

Change your speed evenly and smoothly, both when you are accelerating and when you are slowing down – this is safer and uses less fuel.

Check your speedometer regularly. You might be travelling faster than you think – especially if you are driving in a town or suburb immediately after you have been driving on a higher speed road (such as a dual carriageway).

Slowing down at bends

Dangerous bends and corners are generally indicated by warning signs at the side of the road. These indicate the direction and sharpness of the turn.

As you approach a bend, you need to judge your own speed and decide whether or not you need to slow down. Where the road marking SLOW is shown just in advance of the bend, **it means what it says**.

Reduce your speed in advance of the bend, and then gently accelerate out of the bend. If necessary, change down a gear as you approach sharp bends.

My commitment: 13
I understand the importance of driving at speeds appropriate to the road conditions, and always within the legal speed limits.
Signed (Learner)   Signed (Sponsor)

43

Údarás Um Shábháilteacht Ar Bhóithre
Road Safety Authority

Signalling your intentions

Communicating and cooperating with other road users is very important to road safety. You need to let other road users know what you are about to do, and you need to correctly interpret signals that other drivers give you. The most important signals you can use are your indicators, but in different circumstances, you can also use your horn or hand signals. Your brake lights and reversing lights also help to let other road users know what you're doing.

When to use your indicators

Use your indicator to signal when you intend to:

- Move off or stop;
- Turn (left or right) onto another road and at roundabouts;
- Change lanes;
- Overtake a slower-moving vehicle;
- Move around an obstruction – for example, a bus that has pulled in at a bus stop; and
- Pull into or out of a parking space.

Turn the indicator on soon enough to let other road users know what you are going to do, but not so early that you are likely to cause confusion.

Make the turn when it is safe to do so – just turning on the indicator does not give you the automatic right to turn. For example, when turning right off a main road, you must yield to traffic coming against you; and when turning, you must yield to pedestrians already crossing the road.

There may be situations where you have to be especially careful about when to give the signal – for example, if there are two left turns, one very closely after the other.

Make sure your indicator is turned off after you complete the manoeuvre.

Signalling at the right time. The car has cleared the junction before signalling to turn into the parking space.

For the sponsor

Advice about indicating

Learners can find it difficult to know when to signal in advance of a turn and often they signal too early. Advise the learner about when to signal in advance of a turn.

Advice about hand signals

Explain to the learner the value of hand signals and in what circumstances they are particularly useful. See the *Rules of the Road*.

Brake lights

Every time you put your foot on the brake, your brake lights come on, and this gives vehicles behind you a signal that you are slowing down.

Using your horn

Your car horn is a very important safety device. You can use the horn to warn other road users if you think they haven't seen you. For example, if you see pedestrians at a crossing looking the other way, slow down and (if necessary) use your horn to let them know you are coming.

Don't use your horn aggressively or to tell other people you don't approve of their behaviour.

My commitment: 14
I know when to signal my intentions to other road users – including when to use direction indicators and the horn.

Signed (Learner)	Signed (Sponsor)

Interpreting other road users' intentions

To become a safe and responsible driver, you need to be able to understand other road users' signals. Sometimes you will have to second-guess what other people are going to do. Direction indicators are the easiest to interpret, but you will learn to interpret a wide range of signals, intended and unintended, that other road users give.

Other drivers signal their intentions clearly when they turn on their indicators or apply their brakes. But they also signal their intentions in more subtle ways – for example, by changing speed, by changing lane or changing direction, by pulling in to the side of the road, and so on. Not every driver will signal their intentions clearly.

You need to develop:

- **Skills of observation** … so that you notice subtle changes in other road users' behaviour; and
- **Skills of interpretation** … so that you can correctly interpret what these changes in behaviour mean.

Practice tip

Don't always trust other road users to do the right thing or to do what they say they're going to do – being 'in the right' might not be much consolation if you have a collision. One common mistake that some motorists make is not turning off the indicator after a turn.

For the sponsor

Interpreting other drivers' indicators

A direction indicator on another vehicle means that the vehicle is likely to be changing direction and may also be about to slow down. The learner needs to observe, interpret and react to indicators on other vehicles.

'This driver looks as if she is about to reverse.'

Observation skills (anticipation and reaction)

Developing your skills of observation is a key part of becoming a safe and competent driver. You need to know what's going on around you at all times. Always scan the road ahead for changes in road or traffic conditions before they become dangerous. And the faster you are travelling, the further ahead you will need to look.

Using your mirrors

Your car's mirrors are the 'eyes at the back of your head' that show you what's coming behind. Check your mirrors regularly so you know what's going on, and always check in your mirrors before making any manoeuvre such as changing lanes or turning into a different road.

Remember to check your blind spots before certain manoeuvres – for example, when you are pulling out into traffic from a parking place, or when you are changing lanes.

Because bicycles and motorcycles have such a narrow profile, cyclists can easily become 'hidden' in a blind spot. Be particularly careful to check your blind spot before you open your car door.

Be aware that your side mirrors might have slightly curved glass to give you a wider field of view. This, however, will make things seem to be further away than they actually are.

My commitment: 15
I can interpret other road users' intentions – from the signals they give and also from subtle changes in their behaviour.

| Signed (Learner) | Signed (Sponsor) |

Reversing

Being able to reverse the car accurately is an important skill, and one you should begin to practise while you are still in a safe, traffic-free location.

The steering in your car is controlled by the front wheels. So when you are reversing, the effect of turning the steering wheel is not quite as immediate as when you are going forwards.

Improving your reversing skills is an important part of learning to drive competently. You will need to be able to reverse when you're parking and trying to get out of awkward locations.

Reversing is more difficult than driving forward for the following reasons:

- Your visibility is not as good;
- You're looking over your shoulder; and
- The steering 'feels different'.

Turn around slightly in your seat so that you can see over your shoulder, but also keep an eye out for pedestrians, cyclists or other traffic in front and to the sides. Don't move off until you are satisfied that there is nothing behind the car below the line of your vision. In some circumstances it might be necessary to get out of the car and check that there is no obstruction or hazard that would make reversing dangerous.

Begin by practising to reverse very slowly in a straight line and in a quiet location.

Move on to reversing around corners, both left and right, on level ground and on hills.

Reversing around a corner

As you reverse around a corner, try to keep the rear of the car at roughly the same distance from the kerb throughout the manoeuvre. Make sure the front of your car doesn't swing too far out into the road as you are reversing. Keep checking all around to make sure there are no hazards.

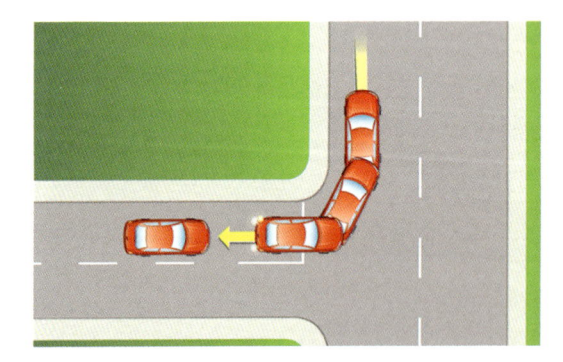

Try to maintain a smooth movement of the car and make sure you have good control of the pedals and the steering as you reverse.

My commitment: 16
I can reverse the car safely and precisely; in a straight line and around corners; and on level ground, uphill and downhill.
Signed (Learner)   Signed (Sponsor)

Parking

To become competent at parking you must be able to manoeuvre the car in confined spaces and at low speed, in both forward and reverse gears.

Car parks

As a learner, you need to be extra careful driving in a car park. You'll probably be driving very slowly but, even so, there are hazards you need to look out for:

- Cars are constantly pulling in and out of parking spaces, often with limited visibility;
- Cars are sharing road space with pedestrians, who are very often accompanied by small children, and who might also be pushing heavy trolleys full of shopping; and
- The standard of road markings in car parks might not be as good as it is on public roads, and the recommended direction of traffic flow might not be clear.

Parking in a bay

In a car park it is usually better to reverse into a parking space. This means that when you are leaving, you can drive out and you won't have to reverse out into the car park traffic. For the same reason, it is also better to reverse into a private entrance or driveway.

1.	Check your mirror and signal your intention to pull into the parking space.
2.	Drive slightly ahead of the space (if possible), giving yourself an easier angle at which to enter the space.
3.	Reverse into the space (either to the left or right).

Keep an eye out all around for pedestrians and for other traffic. Reverse slowly and use your mirrors to check the gap to the cars on either side of the space you are entering. Look forwards to make sure that the front of your car does not touch the cars parked opposite you as you swing into the parking space.

You should aim to park centrally between the lines, so that you don't take up two parking spaces. This will also help ensure that you have enough room to open your door without striking the car parked next to you.

Practice tip

While you are learning, practise parking between the lines in a quiet part of a car park. Or, you could practise manoeuvring the car in tight spaces between cones or other safe obstacles – do this in safe traffic-free environment.

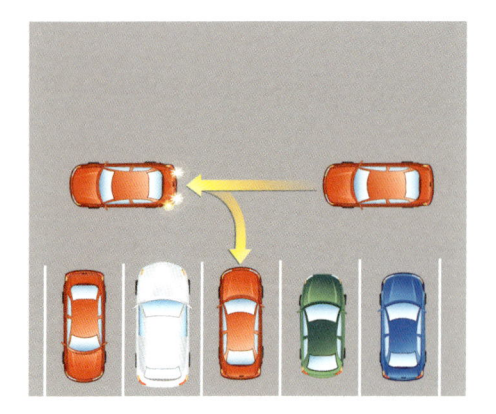

In this example, the driver drives past the space and then reverses at a right angle into the space.

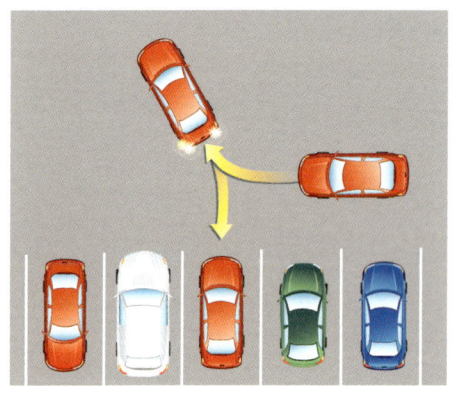

In this example, the driver turns to the right to get an easier angle for reversing into the space. Where there is enough space, this makes the manoeuvre a little easier.

Parking at a kerb

Where there is enough room to do so, you can drive straight into a kerb-side parking space. Check your mirror and signal before you do so.

As you get more confident, you can begin to practise reverse parking between two parked vehicles. You need to be able to do this when there is only one space available. Start by parking in places where the gap between the parked vehicles is at least twice the length of your car. Then, as you get better, you will be able to park where the space is just one and a half time's the length of your car.

It might not be possible to reverse park on a narrow street without holding up the traffic coming behind you while you perform the manoeuvre.

1. Check your mirror and signal your intention to pull into the parking space.
2. Drive slightly ahead of the space so that you are level or slightly ahead of the car in front of the space.
3. Steer to the left to reverse into the space. Keep an eye to the front to ensure that the front of your car does not swing too far into the road, and does not touch the car in front as you come in. Check to the rear to make sure it is safe to reverse and that you do not touch the car behind.
4. Once you are in the space continue to reverse while steering to the right to straighten up.

   Try to leave an equal space to the front and back so that the other cars will have room to manoeuvre out of the spaces they are in.

Practice tip

Reverse parking between two parked cars is a tricky manoeuvre and one that you will need to practise quite a bit before you master it. For practice, choose a quiet location where you won't hold up traffic, and one where the space between the parked cars is ample. The angle at which you approach the parking space is the key to getting it right:

- If the angle is too sharp, your back wheels will touch the kerb before your front wheels are inside the space; and
- If the angle is not sharp enough, your car will end up too far from the kerb.

My commitment: 17

I am able to park the car safely at a kerb (by reversing into a designated space), and in a parking bay in a car park.

Signed (Learner)   Signed (Sponsor)

Overtaking

The ability to overtake slower-moving vehicles safely is one you need to develop. You should always be extremely careful when overtaking on the open road and should always ask yourself these questions:

Is it necessary?	If you are going to turn off the road a few hundred metres further on, or if the vehicle ahead is travelling only slightly slower than you want to go, the answer is probably 'no'.
Is it legal?	In particular, check the road markings. Never cross a continuous white line, except in an emergency. And don't overtake if you would need to exceed the speed limit to do so.
Is it safe?	Make sure the road ahead is clear and you have enough room to overtake and return to your own side of the road. Overtaking a long vehicle while going uphill in a low-powered car might take longer than you think. If in doubt, don't do it. Also make sure that the location is safe – for example, don't overtake at a hump-backed bridge, or at a turn or dip in the road.

To overtake safely, you need to be able to judge the speed of your car, the speed of the vehicle you want to overtake and the speed of other cars – including those coming against you. Don't ever 'take a chance'.

Safe overtaking

The *Rules of the Road* gives detailed advice on how to overtake safely.

Overtaking on the left

You must normally overtake on the right. However, you are allowed to overtake on the left in the following situations:

- You want to go straight ahead, when the driver in front of you has moved out and signalled that they intend to turn right;
- You have signalled that you intend to turn left; or
- Traffic in both lanes is moving slowly and traffic in the left-hand lane is moving more quickly than the traffic in the right-hand lane.

Be aware, however, that other road users might not be expecting to be overtaken on the left, and you might startle them.

Údarás Um Shábháilteacht Ar Bhóithre
Road Safety Authority

My commitment: 18
I am able to overtake slower-moving vehicles.
I will overtake only when it is necessary, legal and safe.

Signed (Learner)	Signed (Sponsor)

Starting on a hill

Learning to start your car on a hill, facing up or down, is an important skill to master.

On a down-hill

Starting on a down-hill is not that difficult, but you do need to be able to control the car as it moves off. Make sure the parking brake (or handbrake) is **on** before you start.

1.	Start the engine.
2.	Press the clutch down fully with your left foot, and put the gear lever into first gear.
3.	Apply the foot brake to hold the car while you release the handbrake. While you are doing this (and while the car is still held in place), signal your intention to move out and check your mirrors and blind spots.
4.	When it is safe to move out, gently release the foot brake. As the car begins to move forward, release the clutch smoothly.
5.	Accelerate gradually and change up into second gear.

Practice tip: When you are learning how to start on a hill, choose a safe and traffic-free environment, so that you can concentrate on the control skills that you need to acquire. Start on the down-hill. When you get to the bottom of the hill, turn around, stop and start again – this time facing uphill.

On an up-hill

Starting on an up-hill is a little bit more tricky, as you need to be able to move the car uphill against its tendency to roll back. To achieve this requires precise and coordinated control of the clutch, accelerator and handbrake.

Make sure the parking brake or handbrake is **on** before you start.

53

Údarás Um Shábháilteacht Ar Bhóithre
Road Safety Authority

1.	Start the engine.
2.	Press the clutch down fully with your left foot, and put the gear lever into FIRST gear.
3.	Very gradually let the clutch pedal up with your left foot while at the same time pressing on the accelerator – usually you will need to press a little more than you would when starting on the flat. You should begin to feel the car slightly resisting the handbrake. While you are doing this, and with the car still held in place, signal your intention to move out and check your mirrors and blind spots.
4.	When it is safe to move out, gently release the handbrake while at the same time releasing the clutch further and pressing on the accelerator.
5.	Once you begin to move, accelerate and change up into second gear.

My commitment: 19

I am able to coordinate and control precisely the clutch, accelerator and handbrake; and I am able to start the car and move off safely on a hill – both downhill and uphill.

Signed (Learner)   Signed (Sponsor)

Turning the car around

Sometimes you have to change the direction you're going in and turn back. You need to learn how to do this safely and competently.

In certain circumstances you can avoid having to turn around on the road – for example, if there is a roundabout ahead, you can drive all the way around it to come back the way you came.

Keep an eye out all around you to make sure it is safe to make the turn.

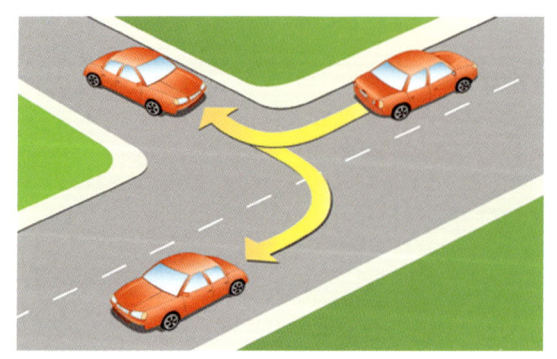

Turning in a side road

If there is a side road near to where you want to turn, you can reverse into it and then drive out.

Practise turning around on quiet side roads before you have to do it on a main road.

Doing a U-turn

Before you do a U-turn, make sure it is safe and legal and that you are not on a one-way street.

Don't attempt a U-turn where it is not permitted.

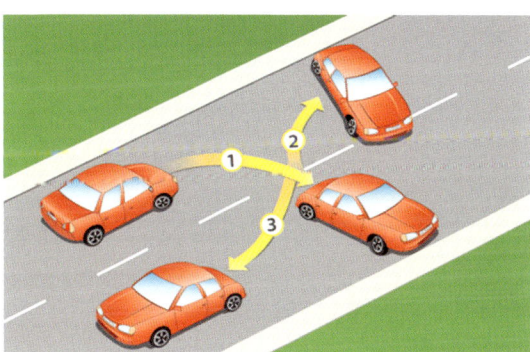

Making a turn-about

This involves turning, reversing and driving off. Depending on how narrow the space is, you might need more than three 'points' to complete this turn.

Before you start, make sure it's safe and legal to turn about.

My commitment: 20
I am able to turn the car around in a confined space – including reverse-and-drive, U-turns and turn-abouts.

Signed (Learner)	Signed (Sponsor)

Stopping in an emergency

In your general driving practice, you need to always expect the unexpected. You literally don't know what's around the next bend, but you can avoid some dangerous situations by developing your observation skills and learning to anticipate danger. Even the best and safest drivers, however, will have to make emergency stops from time to time.

The quicker you respond to a potential emergency, the more likely you are to avert it. So, keep alert and be ready.

In an emergency situation, your objective is to stop as quickly as possible while keeping control of the car:

- If you brake too strongly, the car might skid out of control; and
- If you don't brake strongly enough, the car won't stop in time.

Keep both hands on the steering wheel while you are braking and don't worry about signalling – all your concentration must go on controlling the car and bringing it safely to a stop.

Practice tip

Practising emergency braking

Practise emergency braking in a safe and traffic-free environment. Increase the speed and the braking pressure gradually over a number of practice stops. Your stopping distance also depends on the quality of your tyres, the road surface and whether it is dry or wet. Try to avoid swerving or skidding as you are stopping.

Ask your ADI for advice on how you might control the car in a skid.

My commitment: 21

I will always drive in a safe and responsible manner, and try to anticipate danger. I have practised stopping very quickly as I may need to do this in a real emergency.

Signed (Learner)

Signed (Sponsor)

Driving on motorways

Only drivers with a full driving licence are permitted to drive on motorways, so while you are still a learner you may not practise on a motorway.

You can, however, begin to learn about motorway driving by travelling as a passenger with an experienced driver (such as your sponsor) on a motorway journey. You can observe the points that make motorway driving different from driving on ordinary roads.

After you have passed your driving test and have your full licence, ask your sponsor to accompany you on your first few motorway journeys.

Driving on motorways

The *Rules of the Road* gives comprehensive guidance on motorway driving and also shows examples of the advance signs and warning signs you will meet on the motorway. Revise these sections before your observation journey.

Dealing with fast-moving traffic

Motorways are designed so that traffic can move very freely and at higher speeds than on ordinary national routes (N-roads). Driving in fast-moving traffic in multiple lanes requires total concentration and keen observation. Even the slightest distraction can have very serious consequences.

Motorway driving can also be very monotonous and tiring. Tiredness is a major contributor to motorway collisions. Make sure you are well rested before starting a long motorway journey, and open the window a little every now and then to let in some fresh air.

Knowing where you're going

When you intend to travel on a motorway you need to plan your route much more carefully than you would on N-roads or regional roads – remember, you can't stop and ask for directions on a motorway.

Which exit to take

When you are on the motorway, you need to know which exit to take and you need to get into the correct lane well in advance of the exit. For example, if you are travelling from Portlaoise to Kildare, you leave the M7 at junction 13. Advance information is posted at 2-kilometre and 1-kilometre points ahead of each junction.

This advance direction sign shows that the turn-off for Kildare and Nurney is 1 kilometre away.

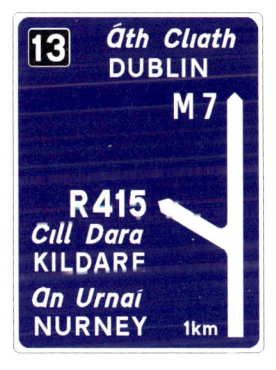

Motorway end points

You also need to know the end point of the motorway you are travelling on. For example, if you are travelling from Thurles to Clonmel, you join the M8 near Cashel and follow the signs for Cork (not Dublin). Clonmel will not be signposted until you get closer to the exit that leads to Clonmel – junction 10, near Cahir.

Údarás Um Shábháilteacht Ar Bhóithre
Road Safety Authority

Getting onto the motorway

Finding your way around motorway junctions can be quite confusing and you can easily lose your bearings. On slip roads, in particular, you might have the feeling that you are going around in circles. For that reason you need to study the direction signs much more carefully than on N-roads, and you need to know the outline of your route in advance.

Points of the compass

In some cases, directions are indicated as points of the compass, so you need to know which direction you are going in.

For example, if you are travelling from Finglas to Drogheda, you join the M50 at Finglas and take the access road marked M50-Northbound Dublin Port.

Similarly, if you are travelling from Finglas to Bray, you join the M50 at Finglas and take the access road marked M50-Southbound Dún Laoghaire.

Getting help with route planning

The Ordnance Survey publishes a range of maps and atlases, including the *Official Road Atlas of Ireland*. There are also many online resources that you can use to help you find the best route to where you want to go.

Your ADI and sponsor will be able to help you with basic route planning.

My commitment: 22

I hold a full category B driving licence, have practised motorway driving and understand the challenges that it presents.

I appreciate the concentration required to drive for prolonged periods at high speed.

I understand the importance of good route planning in advance of beginning a motorway journey.

Signed (Learner)   Signed (Sponsor)

4. Dealing with more challenging conditions

In this chapter

By this stage you have developed your skills as a driver and you have built up considerable 'on the road' experience. You are comfortable behind the wheel and are familiar with most of the situations you are likely to face. You are capable of making the correct decisions in the normal course of driving.

This chapter moves on to look at some of the more challenging conditions that you will face as a driver. Most of these are conditions that you will need to learn about first hand – including driving in heavy traffic, driving at night and driving in bad weather. Other conditions, such as heavy snow or ice, are not that common in Ireland, but you need to know how to handle them when you come across them.

In the course of your practice journeys with your sponsor, you will sometimes meet challenging conditions without warning. For example, there might be a sudden downpour or you might find yourself in traffic coming from a sporting event you didn't know about. In such conditions, the important thing is to keep up the good habits you have already learnt, and just apply them to the changed circumstances. The key skills of observation, judgement, planning and reaction still apply, but you will also need to develop the ability to make the correct decisions independently in challenging conditions or situations.

Combinations of challenging conditions

Challenging conditions can become even more difficult when they come in combination – for example, driving at night in very heavy rain on a very busy national road. Usually, when driving conditions are challenging, you will need to reduce your speed and be even more careful to observe what's going on.

Dealing with hazards

A hazard is anything that requires you to change the position, speed, or direction of your vehicle. For example, a hazard could be a road feature (such as a sharp bend) or the actions of another road user.

As you become more experienced as a driver and become accustomed to a wider variety of road and traffic conditions, you will become better at scanning the road ahead to anticipate and react to the different kinds of hazard that you meet. This will help you to further develop the essential skills of observation, judgement, planning and reaction. The rest of this chapter deals with challenging conditions where you need to make use of these skills.

Údarás Um Shábháilteacht Ar Bhóithre
Road Safety Authority

Driving in heavy traffic

Driving in heavy traffic is not a very pleasant experience. You have to drive a lot slower than normal, it takes longer to get to where you're going, and you use up a lot more fuel stopping and starting and driving in low gears. Also, traffic conditions are unpredictable, which can lead to unexpected delays and frustration. You need to learn how to anticipate and react to changing traffic conditions.

Why is driving in heavy traffic challenging?

In heavy traffic you are likely to be driving at low speeds, and stopping and starting quite a lot – this brings with it a number of challenges. Keep in mind that:

- Your pedal control needs to be very secure – your left foot will spend quite a lot of time on the clutch or hovering just above it;
- You could be 'surrounded' in a middle lane with vehicles, perhaps trucks or buses, on both sides;
- Bicycles and motorcycles might pass on either side of you; and
- Changing lane can be very difficult – you are relying on the courtesy of drivers in other lanes to let you change.

For the sponsor

Advice about heavy traffic

Plan a number of practice journeys in heavy traffic to get the learner used to the challenges that this brings. Don't do so until you feel the learner has the confidence and the driving skills to cope in these conditions.

Other drivers: risks and intimidation

In heavy, slow-moving traffic, some drivers get frustrated – they're late for work or for an appointment, or they just want to get home. Research shows that the highest number of traffic collisions happen during the evening rush, between 4 and 6 o'clock when traffic is at its heaviest.

The biggest challenges you are likely to face in heavy traffic come from other drivers.

- Some drivers may take unnecessary risks, such as changing lanes very suddenly or taking a chance at a level crossing. You need to stay very alert to such changes in behaviour.
- Other drivers may try to intimidate you in various ways (particularly when they see your L-plates) – for example by sounding their horn at you from behind when you stop at an amber light, or when you wait until a box junction is clear before you cross it.

My commitment: 23
I have practised driving in heavy traffic. I am confident that I can control the car, remain patient, and deal with the frustrations of being stuck in traffic.
Signed (Learner)   Signed (Sponsor)

Night-time driving
Why is driving at night challenging?

Your skills of observation depend on what you can actually see, but they also depend on your perception – that is, your awareness and judgement of other factors. For example, you need to be able to judge how far away or how near things are. You need to be able to estimate the speed of other vehicles in relation to your own speed. You also need to be aware of differences in colour and light. Your observation skills also depend on your peripheral vision – that is what you can see out of the corner of your eye. At night, you can see less and therefore you have much less information to help you decide what action to take. This is especially the case when you're driving on unlit rural roads.

Tiredness and other factors at night

You're also more likely to be tired at night, and this will also affect your observation skills as well as your reaction times. There are other factors that can make driving at night challenging. Keep in mind that:

- Traffic is generally much lighter at night, and some drivers are tempted to drive faster than they ought to;
- At night you are much more likely to be sharing the road with drivers whose behaviour is affected by alcohol or tiredness; and
- You can be dazzled both by oncoming and by following drivers who don't dip their main headlights. Even if you're not dazzled, driving against a steady stream of cars with dipped lights can be very tiring and a strain on your eyes which are constantly adjusting between darkness and very bright light.

The *Rules of the Road* gives detailed advice on driving at night.

Some tips for driving safely at night

About a third of all serious road collisions take place at night. This is a very high proportion considering the very low volumes of traffic on the roads at night. For that reason alone, you need to pay extra attention when driving at night, particularly while you are learning.

- You don't necessarily have to drive slower at night; but you do need to moderate your speed to allow for the fact that your perception of possible hazards is limited. If you don't think you could safely bring the car to a stop within the distance of what you can see with your dipped headlights, then you're travelling too fast – slow down!
- Driving at night presents special challenges, especially in unlit places. Headlights from oncoming cars can really affect your night vision. Slow down and maintain a safe course, and avoid looking directly into the headlights of oncoming vehicles. It might take your eyes some time to adjust to different light conditions.
- Think of other drivers and dip your main lights when you see the lights of an oncoming car. You should also dip your lights when you are following another car, to avoid causing mirror dazzle. If you suspect that your lights are not correctly aligned (in other words that even with dipped headlights you are still dazzling oncoming cars), have them checked by a mechanic.

- If you do not already have your dipped headlights on, turn them on at dusk – don't wait for total darkness to fall. This will help other road users to see you.
- It is important that all lights and reflectors are clean and in working order at all times, but this is especially important at night.
- Poor night vision can be a serious traffic hazard. Symptoms include difficulty seeing when driving in the evening or at night, poor vision in reduced light, and feeling that the eyes take longer to 'adjust' to seeing in the dark. If you have concerns about your night vision, seek medical advice.
- Auxiliary lights (extra lights such as fog lights and spot lights) should be used only when appropriate and legal.

Driving in rural areas at night

When driving at night in unlit rural areas, use full beam headlights to give yourself the best view of the road ahead. Even with full beams turned on, you should drive within the limits of what you could see if you were driving with dipped headlights – as you may need to dip your lights suddenly. Make sure to dip your headlights when:

- You meet an oncoming vehicle or other road user; and
- You are closely following another vehicle – your full beams reflecting in the mirror of the car in front can be very dazzling.

Overtaking at night

Avoid overtaking at night unless it's necessary. Take extra care when doing so, as reduced visibility makes it more difficult to judge speed and distance.

My commitment: 24

I have practised driving at night on a variety of different roads, urban and rural. I understand the particular dangers of driving at night and will always drive with consideration for other road users.

Signed (Learner)   Signed (Sponsor)

Practice tip: The purpose of your lights is to help you see and be seen – they're not just for when it's dark, but for any situation where visibility is poor. Turning on your lights does not shorten the life of your battery. Many experienced drivers now drive with dipped headlights or daytime running lights during daylight hours.

Údarás Um Shábháilteacht Ar Bhóithre
Road Safety Authority

Driving in conditions of poor visibility

Any kind of weather that makes it more difficult for you to see what's happening on the road (and makes it more difficult for other road users to see you) presents particular driving challenges, especially for the learner.

Driving in heavy rain

In very heavy rain (or falling snow, hailstones or sleet) your visibility is reduced a good deal. You're looking at the road through a continuous sheet of rain, your wipers are sweeping back and forth, and the cold air outside is likely to cause your windows to mist up. You also have to cope with splashes or spray from passing cars and heavy goods vehicles. And at night-time the wet road surface reflects the lights of oncoming cars and causes glare.

In addition to poor visibility, you need to be aware that a wet road surface does not give your tyres the same level of grip as a dry surface. The road might be particularly slippery when it gets wet after a long spell of dry weather.

What is aquaplaning?

Aquaplaning happens when a car is being driven on a wet road, and a film of water builds up between the tyres and the road surface, so that the tyres are not in direct contact with the road surface.

When the car aquaplanes, the steering will seem very 'loose'. Stay calm, ease off the accelerator to slow the car down, but avoid braking. At a slower speed the water will be dispersed and the tyres will regain their grip on the road surface.

Moderate your speed during heavy rain or where water is building up on the road surface. This will help avoid aquaplaning.

Poor visibility: what can you do?

There are a number of things you can do to make driving safer in heavy rain (or falling snow, hailstones or sleet).

- Turn on your headlights (dipped) so that other drivers can see you more easily.
- Slow down and stay further back from the vehicle in front of you, especially if this is a bus or a heavy goods vehicle that is making a lot of spray. You still need to keep up with the general flow of traffic, but bear in mind that your stopping distance is much greater on wet, greasy roads.
- Be considerate in how you treat other road users in very heavy rain. At least you're inside and dry – pedestrians, cyclists and motorcyclists are not so lucky. Keep in mind that:
    - A pedestrian with an umbrella facing into the wind might not see traffic, and the sound of the rain might also drown out the sound of traffic.
    - When approaching pedestrians and cyclists you should be careful not to splash them as you pass.
    - Cyclists and motorcyclists also have very limited vision in heavy rain and their safe stopping distances are also much greater. Take into account that bicycle brakes don't work very well in wet conditions.
- Brake earlier and more gently than you normally would.

> **Localised flooding**
>
> When you have driven through a large puddle or a flooded area, your brakes may become less effective. In this case, test your brakes to ensure that they have not been affected by the water – check in your mirrors before you do this.
>
> If they have been affected (and this is more than likely just temporary), press gently on the brake pedal as you are driving until they dry out and return to normal.

Údarás Um Shábháilteacht Ar Bhóithre
Road Safety Authority

Driving in fog

Fog is one of the most dangerous weather conditions for all kinds of transport. In dense fog, airports close down and ships stay in port. On the roads, fog can range from being a minor nuisance to being a serious danger.

Fog: what can you do?

Driving in dense fog is not recommended, and you should not travel in foggy conditions unless you really have to. Fog, however, is often quite localised and can come down suddenly without warning. You need to be prepared for it and to know how to behave if you do find yourself in fog. There are a number of things you can do to help make driving in fog safer.

- Make sure to stay a safe distance from the vehicle in front of you, and be satisfied at all times that you can stop within the distance that you can see to be clear.
- Drive at a steady, slow speed. Fog is usually patchy and you will pass through areas where visibility varies. Don't be tempted to speed up through the good patches, as you might find yourself all of a sudden in another dense patch. (Most motorway pile-ups in fog happen when vehicles are driving too fast and too close together.)
- Make sure that other road users can see you. Turn on your headlights (dipped) and fog lights. Don't turn on your main beam headlights as these just beam into the fog and make it more difficult to see where you're going. If the fog is dense, turn on rear fog lights if you have them – but remember to turn them off when the fog is gone.

Driving into a low sun

We usually associate poor visibility with bad weather, but good weather can also cause problems. In particular, you can be dazzled when driving into a low sun (particularly in winter). Keep a pair of sunglasses handy in the car, and use the sun visor to shade your eyes.

The build-up of 'traffic film' on the inside of the windscreen can make it even harder to see when driving into a low sun. Keep the inside and outside of the windscreen clean to avoid the risk of being dazzled.

My commitment: 25
I have practised driving in conditions of poor daytime visibility. I appreciate the importance of both seeing and being seen.

| Signed (Learner) | Signed (Sponsor) |

Driving in poor on-road conditions

In conditions where the road is covered with snow or ice, or is flooded or has patches of loose gravel, your grip on the road can be impaired. In these conditions you are more likely to lose control of the car, especially at higher speeds.

Snow and ice

Snow and ice can make driving very hazardous, and you should avoid making any unnecessary journeys in snow or icy conditions or if these are forecast. If you're not sure, listen to radio broadcasts or warnings from the Road Safety Authority.

Snow and icy conditions can arrive quite suddenly, and you might find yourself driving in snow or ice without expecting to. If conditions become very severe, ask your sponsor to take over driving, and observe how he or she deals with the conditions.

Fresh snow

Freshly fallen snow is not as slippery on the road as ice or compacted snow, and as long as you moderate your speed and keep a good distance from the vehicle in front, you should not have too many problems.

Be aware, however, that fresh snow will cover the road markings and catseyes, including those that mark the edge and the middle of the road. If you are the first car to drive on the fresh snow, you might have difficulty knowing where you are on the road. This will be less of a problem in urban areas where roadside buildings and street furniture will guide you or on busier roads where you can follow the tyre tracks of cars that have gone before you.

You should also watch out for roadside warning signs that might become covered with snow and become more difficult to read. STOP and YIELD signs have distinctive shapes (octagonal and triangular respectively) for that reason.

Compacted snow and ice

Compacted snow that has frozen overnight is particularly treacherous and as it thaws it becomes even more slippery and dangerous. In such conditions, some roads become impassable – for example those with steep hills or with humpbacked bridges. Even where the road has been gritted and salted by the local authority, you need to drive with extreme caution.

Údarás Um Shábháilteacht Ar Bhóithre
Road Safety Authority

Driving through the thaw

As weather conditions improve after a period of snow and frost, it's easy to become complacent, but there are a number of things you should look out for.

- There will be sheltered areas with patches of melting ice that are still very slippery – for example, at bends in the road with overhanging bushes.
- There is a risk of skidding on loose grit spread by the local authorities.
- Melting snow and ice may lead to localised flooding.
- The road surface might have been damaged by the snow and ice, so you need to be on the lookout for potholes and other hazards.
- Where there is a build-up of slush and ice at the sides of the road, cyclists and motorcyclists may have to travel closer to the centre of the road than usual.

Black ice

Black ice is an almost invisible and thin coating of ice on the road surface.

Because it is hard to see, it is particularly dangerous. When the temperature drops close to freezing you can expect to find black ice – particularly in sheltered or shaded areas of the roadway, under trees or beside high walls. Sometimes it can look like a sheet of water or as if the road is wet.

Snow and ice: general advice

- Avoid driving in snowy or icy conditions unless you have to.
- Make sure your tyres have at least the minimum legal tread depth (1.6mm) and are correctly inflated.
- On icy roads, your stopping distance can be up to ten times what it is normally, and it can be very difficult to control the car as you brake. For that reason, you need to:
  - Slow down;
  - Keep your distance from the vehicle in front; and
  - Make sure that all your manoeuvres are smooth and gentle: brake gently and accelerate very gently.
- If your car has ABS or any other advanced driver assistance system, make sure you understand how it works – see your car's user manual.
- Drive in the highest possible gear – this will help you to avoid 'wheel spin'.
- If visibility is poor, turn on your dipped headlights.
- Keep yourself informed about road conditions in times of bad weather – see the RSA website for advice, and listen to radio traffic and weather updates.

Avoiding skids

The most common cause of a skid is driving too fast for the on-road conditions and jerky braking, gear changing or steering. You can reduce the likelihood of skidding by driving smoothly at an appropriate speed, and by keeping your distance from the vehicle in front. Don't rely on your ABS to prevent you from skidding – it won't always do so.

My commitment: 26

I appreciate the dangers of driving in snow and ice and I will not make any unnecessary journeys in such conditions. When I do drive in snow and ice I will drive slower, leave more room ahead, and accelerate and brake smoothly and gently.

Signed (Learner)   Signed (Sponsor)

Dealing with road works and other obstructions

The National Roads Authority and local authorities around the country are continually working to provide a safe and efficient road network and to maintain the quality of road surfaces. Roadworks can vary – they could be major jobs or smaller works, and include the construction of new roads, emergency repairs, routine maintenance of fences and barriers, trimming hedgerows, clearing litter, cutting grass verges, and so on.

When you come across roadworks of any kind, you need to drive with extra care, for your own safety and that of other road users and of the road workers.

Roadworks present challenges to all drivers. These include:

- Detours and different traffic patterns;
- Loose chippings;
- Different lane markers and traffic cones;
- Narrower lanes than usual and restricted shoulder areas;
- Unfinished or very uneven road surfaces;
- Large, slow-moving works vehicles on the road;
- Stop–Go systems or temporary traffic lights; and
- Contraflows on motorways and dual carriageways.

Warning signs

The *Rules of the Road* lists warning signs relating to road works. These signs give warnings, advice and instructions, including information about speed restrictions, detours and road surface conditions. Make sure that you understand what all of these warning signs mean.

Staying safe at roadworks

Follow these easy guidelines to help maintain safety at road works sites:

- Slow down and obey the temporary speed limits posted.
- Obey all the signs, temporary traffic lights and any instructions given to you by flagmen and other road workers.
- Keep a safe distance from the vehicle in front.
- Follow the lane markers and cones (where present).
- Be alert to the movements of road workers and of works traffic.

My commitment: 27

I will always drive through road works with care and consideration. I will obey the warning signs and any instructions given by the road workers.

Signed (Learner)

Signed (Sponsor)

Údarás Um Shábháilteacht Ar Bhóithre
Road Safety Authority

Town and country: challenges of urban and rural driving

Town driving and country driving present very different kinds of challenges. While you are learning to drive, your practice journeys should cover both.

Driving in towns and cities

Driving in towns and cities presents you with a variety of difficult driving situations, often in very quick succession. By this stage in your driving progress you might be reasonably comfortable with complex junctions, multi-lane roundabouts and one-way systems. However, in towns and cities, you will come across these challenges much more often, and they are especially difficult if you are driving in heavy traffic. Hazards you need to be particularly careful about while driving in towns and cities include:

- Obstructions caused by goods vehicles making deliveries;
- Buses pulling in and out at bus stops;
- Cars parked at the side of the street – be careful of doors opening unexpectedly or of children running out from between parked cars;
- More vulnerable road users to consider – including pedestrians and cyclists; and
- Stop-start driving – as the distance between junctions can be quite short.

Urban speed limit

The general speed limit for built-up areas is 50km/h (this might be lower in some areas).

Because of all the hazards in the urban environment, it is particularly important for drivers to have enough time to react, and you should never exceed the speed limit.

My commitment: 28

I have practised driving on urban streets and understand the particular hazards I am likely to come across there. I will always drive within the urban speed limit.

Signed (Learner)   Signed (Sponsor)

Rural driving

Outside of the major urban areas, Ireland has a relatively low density of population served by a very extensive network of roads. To put it in context, Ireland has more than three times the length of road per person than the United Kingdom, and over 80% of Irish roads are local roads. In country areas, most roads were in place before motor vehicles were invented and are narrow and winding. This can present particular challenges to drivers – with more collisions occurring on rural roads than on urban roads.

Other road users

On country roads you are more likely to meet slow-moving vehicles, such as tractors and other agricultural vehicles. Don't try to overtake these vehicles unless you have a clear view of the road ahead and the road is wide enough to overtake safely. Be patient: they are probably travelling only a very short distance. Many narrow country roads do not have central road markings and allow very little room for two vehicles to pass.

You are more likely to meet livestock on country roads. Be prepared to slow down or stop and don't do anything to frighten the animals.

Visibility

High hedges and the winding nature of country roads can impair visibility – blind corners, sharp bends and dips in the road can be particularly dangerous. You should always adjust your speed to suit the road you are driving on and you must never exceed the speed limit. In many cases, a safe speed might be much less than the stated speed limit for the road. You need to be able to stop the car in the road space that you can see – if you can't, you're driving too fast.

Make sure you heed warnings to slow down and warning signs for dangerous bends or corners.

Road surface

Local authorities give priority to maintaining roads with heavier traffic, so country roads with less traffic might not have the same surface quality. Also, on country roads watch out for loose gravel, mud and things like fallen leaves on the road – all of these can make the surface slippery, especially after rain.

My commitment: 29

I have practised driving on country roads and I understand that visibility might be poor and that the road surfaces might be more uneven than on urban or national roads. While driving on country roads I will be considerate to the needs of farmers and other country dwellers and their animals.

Signed (Learner)　　　　　　　　　　　Signed (Sponsor)

5. Sharing the road

In this chapter

The basic skills of driving are not that difficult to master, and with a good ADI, a patient sponsor and a well-planned schedule of driving practice, you can be competent in all the major skills before long. At this stage, you've probably also begun to realise that the experience of driving is really one of sharing the road responsibly with other people. Learning to do that is much more difficult, and you need to:

- Be in good physical and mental condition to drive safely and competently;
- Stay calm even if other drivers are behaving badly, and not allow your own emotions to get the better of you;
- Avoid distractions while driving but learn to deal with those that do arise;
- Behave with consideration and courtesy to other road users, including pedestrians, cyclists, motorcyclists and drivers of larger vehicles;
- Consider how you can reduce the impact of your driving on the environment; and
- Know what to do if you arrive at the scene of a collision.

Making sure you're fit to drive

Medical conditions

Some medical conditions can have an effect on driving. Even a bad cold or a simple viral infection can increase your reaction time and lower your concentration levels. If you are being treated for any medical condition, ask your doctor if it is safe for you to drive.

Facts about alcohol and drugs

- Drink-driving is a factor in about a quarter of all fatal collisions in Ireland.
- Across Europe, alcohol or drugs are a factor in almost a quarter of all collisions, leading to about 10,000 deaths a year.

The effects of alcohol: never ever drink and drive

Driving while under the influence of alcohol puts you at a much greater risk of being involved in a collision. Collisions caused by drink-driving are usually preventable. **Never, ever drink and drive.** It's not worth the risk, either to yourself or to other road users.

Alcohol slows down your nervous system and causes you to function less effectively in many different ways. In summary, alcohol:

- Impairs your vision and reduces your 'field of vision' – in particular your peripheral vision (what you see out of the corner of your eye);
- Impairs your perception – your ability to judge how far away objects are, including other cars;
- Makes it more difficult for you to coordinate the various tasks that driving involves – steering, braking, observing road signs, and so on;
- Dulls your reflexes so that you are no longer able to react quickly in dangerous situations. In other words, your reaction time is much longer and your physical movements (for example, putting your foot on the brake) are much slower; and
- Causes loss of judgement, give you false confidence and a lack of inhibition in relation to speed, which in turn leads to drivers 'taking a chance'.

The effects of other drugs

Drugs (legal and illegal) can impair your ability and change the way you drive. For example, drugs such as depressants dull your reactions, while stimulants heighten your senses and can make you overreact.

- Depressants (or downers) have similar effects to alcohol and are particularly dangerous when taken with alcohol. Prescribed depressants include tranquillisers for relief of anxiety and tension.
- Narcotics include some legally prescribed pain-killers and illegal drugs such as heroin and cannabis. Their effects include euphoria (feeling unnaturally happy), giddiness and drowsiness.
- Hallucinogenic drugs lead to nausea and affect your perception – which is especially dangerous considering how important perception is to a driver. This category of drugs includes Ecstasy and LSD.
- Stimulants are used medicinally to increase alertness and to relieve tiredness. They can also cause hyperactivity, aggressiveness and reckless behaviour – all of which impair your ability to drive safely.

If you are taking any kind of medication, prescribed or over-the-counter, ask your doctor or pharmacist to confirm that it's OK to drive.

Údarás Um Shábháilteacht Ar Bhóithre
Road Safety Authority

The effects of tiredness

Tiredness is one of the main causes of serious road collisions. When you're very tired, you are much less alert, have poorer physical coordination and your reaction times are much slower. You will also find it more difficult to 'read the road' and take in direction signs, warning signs and other information as you drive. You also run the very grave risk of dozing off at the wheel, with potentially fatal consequences.

You are more likely to become tired when driving on main roads with low traffic volumes (particularly on motorways), where the driving task is fairly monotonous and there is very little stimulation. Other conditions that can lead to tiredness include driving:

- In traffic jams or very slow-moving traffic;
- In the rain – when the windscreen wipers can have a hypnotic effect; and
- At night, when you would normally be asleep.

Avoiding and handling tiredness

The best way to handle tiredness is to avoid it in the first place – in particular, make sure you are well rested in advance of a longer journey. Tea or coffee can help some people, but do not depend on them to keep away tiredness. There are some things you can do to avoid and handle tiredness:

- On longer trips, take a 15-minute break at least once in every two hours of driving: get some fresh air and stretch your legs; and
- If possible, share the driving with someone else.

Údarás Um Shábháilteacht Ar Bhóithre
Road Safety Authority

My commitment: 30

I will drive only when I am physically fit to do so.

I will never, ever drink and drive.

I will never, ever drive while under the influence of drugs (legal or illegal)

Signed (Learner)   Signed (Sponsor)

Staying calm: showing courtesy

There are so many things that can stress you when you are driving: heavy traffic, bad weather, road works, waiting at level crossings, other drivers' bad behaviour – all of these can build up frustration and make it difficult for you to stay calm and focus on arriving safely at your destination. Your own emotional state can also play a big part in how well you drive. If you are worried or upset, angry or depressed, it will probably show in your driving.

You can help to reduce stress by giving yourself enough time to get to your destination without feeling rushed. Don't allow yourself to become impatient, as this can lead to rash behaviour and taking unnecessary risks. Cooperate with other road users and remain courteous and tolerant in your dealings with them, particularly with more vulnerable road users such as pedestrians and cyclists. If you need to, take a short break to compose yourself before you get into the car. If you're late for an appointment, accept the fact – stop the car in a safe place and phone ahead to tell the person expecting you that you'll be a little late.

Annoying actions to avoid

Think about your own driving practice. Are there things you do that could annoy other drivers or other road users? The most common annoying actions (some of which are illegal) include:

- Tailgating – driving too close to the car in front;
- Signalling very late before turning – the cars behind might not be able to move around you;
- Not dipping your main headlights when you meet oncoming vehicles or when driving behind another vehicle;
- Passing on the inside in fast-moving traffic;
- Driving in the outer lane of a dual carriageway or motorway (other than when overtaking);
- Aggressive use of the horn;
- Weaving in and out of traffic lanes; and
- Slowing down for no apparent reason or driving significantly below the speed limit for no good reason.

Other drivers' behaviour

Some drivers seem to think of driving as a kind of competitive sport, and don't show much consideration for other road users. They may cut inside you, indicate at the last minute, blare their horn, make aggressive gestures, and so on.

This kind of aggressive behaviour can very easily turn into 'road rage' where people who are normally civil and courteous lose self-control and act very irresponsibly when they feel themselves 'provoked'. Don't allow yourself to be drawn into this kind of situation. Let such drivers go ahead – you will be safer if you are not in their vicinity.

Good drivers stay patient, courteous and tolerant at all times and don't respond to provocation – they know that they'll get there just as quickly if they ignore such actions. 'Count to ten' and give yourself time to cool down.

My commitment: 31
I understand the importance of remaining calm, patient and courteous at all times while driving.
I will not allow myself to be 'provoked' by the behaviour of other road users.
Signed (Learner)   Signed (Sponsor)

Avoiding and dealing with distractions while driving

As you know by now, driving requires you to take in a great deal of information – about other traffic, road conditions, direction and warning signs, and so on. Just dealing with that amount of information is quite enough, and you don't need to add to the load by letting yourself be distracted. A distraction is anything that takes away your concentration while you are driving; and when you are distracted, your reactions will be slower and your judgement will not be as good. It is an offence to drive 'without due care and attention'.

Mobile phones

Using a hand-held mobile phone (or one without a hands-free kit) while driving is an offence. It is unsafe because it prevents you from concentrating fully on driving. It is illegal to hold a mobile phone in your hand or to support it on your shoulder.

Using a hands-free phone kit is not illegal, but in some circumstances it could be a dangerous distraction, and you could be prosecuted for dangerous driving, careless driving or driving without due care and attention.

If you have to make a call, find a safe, legal and convenient place to stop.

Maintaining concentration

Good drivers concentrate and keep their mind on the task in hand at all times. They don't allow distractions of any kind to interfere with their number one priority when driving – to arrive safely at their destination. Things that can take from your concentration and distract your attention from the road include:

- Lighting and smoking cigarettes;
- Adjusting the radio or CD player;
- Personal grooming activities such as shaving, applying lipstick or other make-up;
- Using in-car systems, such as multi-function displays;
- Programming a sat-nav;
- Eating or drinking; and
- Passenger distractions – for example, boisterous children.

Young drivers and peer pressure

Young drivers (particularly young men), are inclined to drive faster, pay less attention to the road and are more likely to take chances when their friends are in the car. You need to be aware of these risks and to take responsibility for ensuring that you and your passengers have a safe journey.

For any young person, becoming a competent driver is a big step towards maturity and you need to show in your driving behaviour that you are mature enough to resist any peer pressure to drive faster or to take risks. If your friends are passengers in the car, make sure that they:

- Wear their seatbelts – every passenger must have their own seatbelt;
- Do nothing to distract you from driving;
- Make no movements that could destabilise the car on the road; and
- Do not make any comments on your driving or put any pressure on you.

Do not overload the car – never carry more passengers than you have seatbelts for.

My commitment: 32
I will not do anything that will distract me from my driving.
I will not respond or react to distractions caused by others.

Signed (Learner)	Signed (Sponsor)

Údarás Um Shábháilteacht Ar Bhóithre
Road Safety Authority

Dealing with other road users

As a driver you share the road with other drivers and with many other people as well: cyclists, motorcyclists, pedestrians, bus drivers and truck drivers, and in rural areas you can sometimes meet farm animals. You need to cooperate with other road users and be conscious at all times of the different view of the road that they might have. And you also need to understand your own responsibilities.

Pedestrians

Pedestrians are among the most vulnerable road users, and you should always slow down when driving in an area where there is a lot of pedestrian traffic. You should be especially alert to the safety of small children – for example, if you're driving near schools. You also need to watch out for elderly people who might not always manage to cross the road before the traffic light changes.

Most rural roads do not have footpaths and pedestrians have to walk on the margin of the road, however unsuitable that might be. For example, in wet weather the road margin might be very soft or muddy underfoot. Slow down if you see pedestrians on either side of the road ahead – don't expect them to move into the ditch.

You can expect to find higher numbers of pedestrians:

- At and near bus stops;
- At the entrances to railway stations;
- Near schools at opening and closing times;
- Around sports venues;
- Along popular jogging routes;
- Near hospitals; and
- On shopping streets.

Joining a main road

If you are joining a main road from a side road you should give way to pedestrians on the main road who are crossing the side road.

If you are emerging from a private entrance, you should give way to pedestrians on the margin of the road or on the footpath (if there is one).

Note

Emergency service vehicles

If you hear or see a Garda or emergency vehicle approaching under emergency conditions and using a siren or flashing lights, you should exercise caution and give way if it is safe to do so. Never 'tailgate' an emergency vehicle.

Vulnerable road users

Watch out for disabled people and other vulnerable road users – including blind and visually impaired pedestrians (with or without guide dogs). Remember that some pedestrians might be deaf or hard of hearing and might not hear you coming.

Be careful when passing drivers of powered wheelchairs or other vehicles used by people with disabilities.

Cyclists

Cyclists are just as entitled to use the road as you are, and you need to pay special attention to them.

- Cyclists can sometimes make sudden movements – for example, to avoid a pothole or some broken glass or other objects on the road.
- In bad weather cyclists have less control – they could be blown off balance by strong winds and they can find it difficult to see in heavy rain. Also, they could skid very easily in icy conditions.
- At night, cyclists are more difficult for drivers to see. Even if they have good lights and reflective clothing, cyclists can get 'lost' in the glare of much stronger car lights.
- When you are passing a cyclist, make sure you leave enough room between your car and the cyclist. The faster you are travelling, the more space you should leave. Avoid passing a cyclist if the road is too narrow – slow down and wait for a wider stretch of road.
- Check your blind spots for cyclists when you manoeuvre in traffic, especially before you pull out into traffic from a parking space.

81

- If you are turning left, you should give way to cyclists on your inside who are going straight on or turning left. This applies whether or not there is a marked cycle lane. This also applies on roundabouts where you should not cut across a cyclist to make your exit.
- Do not drive or park on a cycle lane.
- Be particularly careful dealing with children on bicycles, as they might not have very good road sense or control of their bicycles.
- If traffic is moving slowly, cyclists may overtake you on the inside. Always check your mirrors and your blind spots before turning or pulling into the kerb.

Motorcyclists

Many of the things you need to remember about cyclists also apply to motorcyclists. Like cyclists they are also very vulnerable and can easily become 'hidden' in a blind spot or behind a larger vehicle or other obstacles. Because they travel so much faster than cyclists, dangerous situations can arise much more quickly.

- Always look out for motorcyclists when you are coming out of a parking space or a private entrance.
- Due to its small size, a motorcycle may seem further away than it actually is, and it may be difficult to judge its speed.
- Keep your distance when travelling behind a motorcycle.
- Watch out for motorcyclists riding between lanes in very slow-moving traffic.

Farm traffic

In rural areas you can expect to meet tractors and other slow-moving agricultural machinery as well as cattle and sheep being herded along the road.

- Be patient if you are behind a tractor and cannot pass.
- Slow down if you meet animals being herded along the road or if you meet people on horseback. Don't use your horn, as this might frighten the animals.

In more remote areas of open countryside, you might meet sheep on the road or grazing along the roadside. Slow down until you have passed them, as they are easily frightened and not always predictable in their movements.

Larger vehicles

Driving a truck or bus is not an easy job, especially on some of our narrower urban streets and regional roads. The particular problems that truck and bus drivers have are mostly related to the size of their vehicles. As a car driver, you can help to make their job a little easier if you take the following into account.

Blind spots	All vehicles have some blind spots, and the bigger the vehicle the bigger the blind spots are. If you are driving behind a truck and you cannot see the truck's mirror, then the truck driver cannot see you. Truck cabs tend to be quite high above the road, so the space immediately in front of the truck at ground level is also a blind spot.
Turning room	Trucks and buses usually need to swing quite wide to the right before they make a left turn. Do not attempt to pass a truck or bus on the inside when it is turning left – you could end up being caught between the truck and the kerb.
Reversing	Trucks and buses sometimes have to reverse into quite restricted spaces – this is especially true for trucks delivering goods. Don't cross behind a large vehicle while it is reversing.
Bus stops	Passenger buses stop frequently to set down and take on passengers, and you should be careful of pedestrians in the vicinity of bus stops. You should give way to a bus that is signalling its intention to rejoin the stream of traffic.

My commitment: 33

I will treat all other road users with courtesy and respect, particularly more vulnerable road users such as pedestrians, cyclists and motorcyclists.

Signed (Learner)   Signed (Sponsor)

› Údarás Um Shábháilteacht Ar Bhóithre
Road Safety Authority

Thinking of the environment

The motor industry is making substantial efforts to reduce the environmental damage caused by driving. Modern cars are generally much more efficient in their use of fuel, have lower greenhouse gas emissions, and cause less pollution.

As a driver, you can also do quite a lot to reduce your personal carbon footprint and to minimise the impact your driving has on the environment.

Fuel-efficient driving

There are a number of simple steps you can take to make your driving more fuel-efficient, and save you money. Drivers who follow these steps are also safer drivers.

Drive smoothly

For greater fuel efficiency, speed up gradually, slow down gradually, and drive smoothly in as high a gear as possible.

- The faster you accelerate, the more fuel you use and there is often very little point in accelerating away from one traffic light to meet a red light at the next.
- Revving or racing your engine while you wait at traffic lights is a waste of fuel.
- Less stopping and starting is more economical.

Reduce your speed

On main roads and motorways, the faster you drive the more fuel you are using. For example, a car travelling at 120km/h uses up to 20% more fuel than the same car travelling at 100km/h; and on a 20km journey, the time saving would be only two minutes. Can you afford to be in such a hurry?

Avoid unnecessary idling

If you're stopping for more than 30 seconds or so (except in traffic), turn off the engine.

Service your car regularly

Service your car regularly to ensure that you get the best performance and best fuel efficiency. Simple changes such as replacing worn spark plugs and clogged air filters can save fuel consumption by up to 10%.

Check your tyre pressure regularly

Check your tyre pressure regularly and make sure that you follow the manufacturer's guidelines for your car. Under-inflated tyres drag more on the road so your engine has to work harder and uses more fuel. Over-inflating your tyres can be dangerous, as they will then have less grip on the road.

Reduce your load

The greater the weight in your car, the more fuel the engine uses. Clear out your boot every now and then to make sure you're not carrying around any unnecessary items.

Roof racks and boxes reduce your car's aerodynamic efficiency and add to fuel consumption. Take them off when you no longer need them.

Use the air conditioning sparingly

Your car's air conditioning system runs off the engine, which means that your car uses more fuel when the air conditioning is turned on – up to ten per cent more, depending on how cool you want to be and on the efficiency of the system.

Take advantage of fuel economy technology

Some cars have a computerised monitor that reports on fuel economy, usually by way of a dashboard display. Such monitors keep you informed about your fuel consumption, and you can use the feedback to improve your driving habits and achieve better fuel economy.

Drive less and plan ahead

Is your trip really necessary? Could you walk or use public transport? Could you combine a number of trips into one? Is there a better time of day for a particular trip? Would a car with a smaller engine suit your needs just as well?

In urban areas and at certain times of the day, a very high percentage of car journeys are very short and in heavy traffic. It can sometimes be much quicker to use an alternative form of transport.

Eco-friendly vehicles

Eco-friendly vehicles such as those that use hybrid or electric technology have lower emissions than vehicles powered only by petrol or diesel. Over the lifetime of the car, the savings in emissions can be quite substantial.

Hybrids have particularly low emissions at low speeds or while stopped at traffic lights or in city traffic jams, so your emissions savings can be considerable if most of your driving is low-speed city driving.

My commitment: 34

I accept that driving has an impact on the environment. I will try to minimise that impact by the way that I use my car and the way that I drive.

Signed (Learner)   Signed (Sponsor)

Disposing of car waste

Many of the parts and fluids that your car uses are regarded as 'hazardous waste' when they come to the end of their usefulness. These parts and fluids include engine oil, brake fluid, transmission fluid, antifreeze fluid, oil filters, batteries and so on.

If you do your own car servicing, make sure that you bring all your waste to a recycling centre or to a specialised hazardous waste recycling company licensed by the Environmental Protection Agency.

Disposing of car maintenance waste in any other way is illegal and very damaging to the environment, and you could be prosecuted.

Disposing of your car

When a car comes to the end of its life, it must be disposed of in a controlled manner to ensure that it does not pose any threat to the environment. There are authorised treatment facilities around the country that are licensed to perform this service without charge. Contact your local authority or a main dealer for your make of car for further information.

My commitment: 35

I understand the hazardous nature of car waste and will never dispose of any waste except through licensed recycling centres.

Signed (Learner)   Signed (Sponsor)

Dealing with collisions and emergencies

Arriving at the scene of a collision

If you are the first to arrive at the scene of a traffic collision, there are a number of guidelines you need to follow:

- Stay calm, stop, apply the handbrake, put the car into neutral gear, switch off the engine, and assess the situation.
- Call the emergency services on 112 or 999. Don't assume that other people at the scene of the collision have already done that. Give the emergency services precise information about the nature of the collision, its location, and how many people you think are injured.
- Warn others about the collision.
  - By turning on your hazard lights
  - By placing a warning triangle on the road a good distance from the site of the collision (if safe to do so); and
  - By any other means you think necessary
- Do not do anything to endanger your own safety. Make sure you are safe yourself before attending to other people, and put on a hi-vis jacket if you have one. Place coats or rugs over anyone who is injured to keep them warm, but do not give them anything to eat or drink.
- Do not move an injured person unless there is a real danger of fire or of a vehicle turning over. Do not remove helmets from injured motorcyclists. Do not try to lift a vehicle off an injured person without help.
- If you have time, draw a sketch or take photographs of the collision – these may be useful to the authorities investigating how the collision happened.

If you arrive at the scene of a collision and the emergency services are already there, drive on carefully and do not stop unless directed to do so.

Reporting a collision

If you are involved in a collision in which anybody is injured, you must report it to An Garda Síochána, either to a garda at the scene or at a Garda station. If there is no garda at the scene, you must give your personal and vehicle details, including insurance details, to anyone involved in the collision and also to any independent witness who asks for this information.

My commitment: 36	
If I am ever the first to arrive at the scene of a collision, I will respond quickly, calmly and responsibly and I will do nothing to further endanger the health or safety of anyone.	
Signed (Learner)	Signed (Sponsor)

Summary of commitments

My commitment: 1

I understand the responsibility of taking a car onto the road and of sharing the road with other people. I am ready to take on that personal responsibility and to take ownership of how I learn to drive.

Signed (Learner)   Signed (Sponsor)

My commitment: 2

I am willing to learn how to drive in a structured and controlled way with the help of my sponsor and my ADI.

Signed (Learner)   Signed (Sponsor)

My commitment: 3

I understand the legal issues relating to driving a car and I commit myself to safe and responsible practice.

Signed (Learner)   Signed (Sponsor)

My commitment: 4

I understand how important it is to maintain my car in a safe and roadworthy condition. I have a good understanding of the basic service and maintenance requirements of my car, and I know how to carry out basic checks myself.

Signed (Learner)   Signed (Sponsor)

My commitment: 5

I know what to do when I first sit into the driver's seat of a car. I can operate all the manual controls without taking my eyes off the road.

Signed (Learner)   Signed (Sponsor)

My commitment: 6

I am able to start the car, drive a few metres and stop the car in a safe, traffic-free location.

Signed (Learner)　　　　　　　　　　Signed (Sponsor)

My commitment: 7

I am able to drive the car in a traffic-free location and can change gears.

Signed (Learner)　　　　　　　　　　Signed (Sponsor)

My commitment: 8

I am able to drive the car on the public road in a quiet location in very light traffic.

Signed (Learner)　　　　　　　　　　Signed (Sponsor)

My commitment: 9

I understand the importance of planning my practice journeys in advance and reviewing them afterwards with my sponsor.

Signed (Learner)　　　　　　　　　　Signed (Sponsor)

My commitment: 10

I am able to 'read the road' – to take in the information I need from road markings, regulatory and warning signs, traffic lights, and direction signs.

Signed (Learner)　　　　　　　　　　Signed (Sponsor)

My commitment: 11

I know how to position my car on the road. I keep a safe distance between my car and the vehicle ahead; I understand how lanes work and can position my car in the appropriate lane at all times while driving.

Signed (Learner)　　　　　　　　　　Signed (Sponsor)

My commitment: 12

I can safely negotiate all types of road junction – including left and right turns (from major to minor and from minor to major roads), slip roads, junctions with traffic lights, and roundabouts.

Signed (Learner)

Signed (Sponsor)

My commitment: 13

I understand the importance of driving at speeds appropriate to the road conditions, and always within the legal speed limits.

Signed (Learner)

Signed (Sponsor)

My commitment: 14

I know when to signal my intentions to other road users – including when to use direction indicators, the horn and flashing headlights.

Signed (Learner)

Signed (Sponsor)

My commitment: 15

I can interpret other road users' intentions – from the signals they give and also from subtle changes in their behaviour.

Signed (Learner)

Signed (Sponsor)

My commitment: 16

I can reverse the car safely and precisely; in a straight line and around corners; and on level ground, uphill and downhill.

Signed (Learner)

Signed (Sponsor)

My commitment: 17

I am able to park the car safely at a kerb (by reversing into a designated space), and in a parking bay in a car park.

Signed (Learner)

Signed (Sponsor)

My commitment: 18

I am able to overtake slower-moving vehicles.

I will overtake only when it is necessary, legal and safe.

Signed (Learner)　　　　　　　　　　Signed (Sponsor)

My commitment: 19

I am able to coordinate and control precisely the clutch, accelerator and handbrake; and I am able to start the car and move off safely on a hill – both downhill and uphill.

Signed (Learner)　　　　　　　　　　Signed (Sponsor)

My commitment: 20

I am able to turn the car around in a confined space – including reverse-and-drive, U-turns and turn-abouts.

Signed (Learner)　　　　　　　　　　Signed (Sponsor)

My commitment: 21

I will always drive in a safe and responsible manner, and try to anticipate danger. I have practised stopping very quickly as I may need to do this in a real emergency.

Signed (Learner)　　　　　　　　　　Signed (Sponsor)

My commitment: 22

I hold a full category B driving licence, have practised motorway driving and understand the challenges that it presents.

I appreciate the concentration required to drive for prolonged periods at high speed.

I understand the importance of good route planning in advance of beginning a motorway journey.

Signed (Learner)　　　　　　　　　　Signed (Sponsor)

My commitment: 23

I have practised driving in heavy traffic. I am confident that I can control the car, remain patient, and deal with the frustrations of being stuck in traffic.

Signed (Learner)   Signed (Sponsor)

My commitment: 24

I have practised driving at night on a variety of different roads, urban and rural. I understand the particular dangers of driving at night and will always drive with consideration for other road users.

Signed (Learner)   Signed (Sponsor)

My commitment: 25

I have practised driving in conditions of poor daytime visibility. I appreciate the importance of both seeing and being seen.

Signed (Learner)   Signed (Sponsor)

My commitment: 26

I appreciate the dangers of driving in snow and ice and I will not make any unnecessary journeys in such conditions. When I do drive in snow and ice I will drive slower, leave more room ahead, and accelerate and brake smoothly and gently.

Signed (Learner)   Signed (Sponsor)

My commitment: 27

I will always drive through road works with care and consideration. I will obey the warning signs and any instructions given by the road workers.

Signed (Learner)   Signed (Sponsor)

My commitment: 28

I have practised driving on urban streets and understand the particular hazards I am likely to come across there. I will always drive within the urban speed limit.

Signed (Learner)

Signed (Sponsor)

My commitment: 29

I have practised driving on country roads and I understand that visibility might be poor and that the road surfaces might be more uneven than on urban or national roads. While driving on country roads I will be considerate to the needs of farmers and other country dwellers and their animals.

Signed (Learner)

Signed (Sponsor)

My commitment: 30

I will drive only when I am physically fit to do so.

I will never, ever drink and drive.

I will never, ever drive while under the influence of drugs (legal or illegal)

Signed (Learner)

Signed (Sponsor)

My commitment: 31

I understand the importance of remaining calm, patient and courteous at all times while driving.

I will not allow myself to be 'provoked' by the behaviour of other road users.

Signed (Learner)

Signed (Sponsor)

My commitment: 32

I will not do anything that will distract me from my driving.

I will not respond or react to distractions caused by others.

Signed (Learner)

Signed (Sponsor)

My commitment: 33

I will treat all other road users with courtesy and respect, particularly more vulnerable road users such as pedestrians, cyclists and motorcyclists.

| Signed (Learner) | Signed (Sponsor) |

My commitment: 34

I accept that driving has an impact on the environment. I will try to minimise that impact by the way that I use my car and the way that I drive.

| Signed (Learner) | Signed (Sponsor) |

My commitment: 35

I understand the hazardous nature of car waste and will never dispose of any waste except through licensed recycling centres.

| Signed (Learner) | Signed (Sponsor) |

My commitment: 36

If I am ever the first to arrive at the scene of a collision, I will respond quickly, calmly and responsibly, and will do nothing to further endanger the health or safety of anyone.

| Signed (Learner) | Signed (Sponsor) |